GW00777406

John Montague

One morning in 1917, Henri Matisse threw open the shutters of his hotel room in Nice and marvelled at a sea 'the blue of sapphires, of the peacock's wing... and yet it is none of these, for it shines with the unearthly radiance of Neptune's kingdom'. My wife, Elizabeth, and I experienced a similar excitement when we first glimpsed the sea at Nice, only it was from the window not of a room but of a plane. Matisse had journeyed into the blue radiance of Nice from the pewter light of northern France, and we also were arriving from the north of Europe, though from grey Belfast, where I was teaching at Queen's University during my first term as the first Ireland Professor of Poetry. When the wing tilted over the Bay of Angels, and the light seemed to flare up to greet us, we fell in love with the French Riviera.

Speaking of angels, it sometimes seems that the Angel of Art (like Chagall's tender angels in the Nice museum that bears his name) flies over a place and briefly anoints it with genius. Florence, Paris and Vienna all flourished with extraordinary artists for a blessed period before the Angel floated onwards to sprinkle its gold dust on yet another region. For a time, that region was the Côte d'Azur. In *An Art Lover's Guide to the French Riviera*, Patrick J. Murphy observes, 'The magic of the French Riviera is hard to define'. But he makes a noble effort, describing the intensely blue yet slightly silver light that dazzled Matisse, along with the snow-topped Maritime Alps, and the flowers 'musky in the gentle heat'.

Murphy clearly loves the Côte d'Azur and its artists past and present, so much so that this book transforms the Riviera into one vast treasure house. It is a paean not only to the region's fifty major museums and large commercial galleries, but to churches where little-known masterpieces are housed, obscure galleries along crooked passageways, flea markets, public sculptures and architecture.

The author's passion for his subject shows in the quality of his research and in the erudite clarity with which he presents the material gathered in this book. Full of loving detail, intelligent reflection and practical information, it provides us with hundreds of opportunities to view art along the Riviera, 'from open-air museums in bustling cities to the remotest of hilltop villages'.

The author is a seasoned art collector whose other career, as a malt-exporter, took him all around the world, but 'nowhere struck [him] as more beautiful or interesting than the French Riviera'. Sensibly, he and his wife bought an apartment in Nice, a city full of artistic splendour which also serves as 'an ideal base from which to investigate the equally rich artistic hinterland'.

One of this book's singular charms is how it draws us not only through space but into history. Walking with *An Art Lover's Guide* through the opulent Hotel Negresco, we regard a portrait of the Sun King and then 'a most attractive bronze bust of portly Madame Renoir by her husband'. And after that, Niki de Saint Phalle's madcap, three-metre high, multicoloured *La Nana Jaune*, made in 1995. And since *An Art Lover's Guide* is peppered with wonderful anecdotes, we learn of Saint Phalle and her husband shooting at canisters of paint to make 'spectacular...splashes', an event which the author hopes was carefully arranged in front of an invited audience who were instructed to stand at a prudent distance to avoid being shot (in Technicolor).

In Nice alone, we are given a tour of the renowned Modern Art Museum (MAMAC) and the Musée Masséna, but also of the less well-known Galerie des Ponchettes, the Galerie de la Marine, and Rifaldi's, a mysterious commercial gallery deep in the warrens of Old Nice. It is lovely to read Murphy's meticulous descriptions of the Matisse and Chagall Museums, and of the Fine Arts Museum with its splendid Bronzino whose surface looks 'almost metallic or enamelled'. I was especially delighted to learn that the Fine Arts Museum also contains a Bastien-Lepage, whose haunting Joan of Arc hangs in the Metropolitan Museum of Art in New York.

In *An Art Lover's Guide to the French Riviera*, we find the limpid religious paintings of fifteenth-century local master Louis Brea, along with the contemporary open-air art of Jaume Plensa, whose crouching forms adorn Nice's Place Massena. We journey from St-Tropez, through Cannes, and Antibes with its wonderful Picasso Museum, to Nice and eastwards to the border of Italy, sampling treasures all along the way. This book, a labour of love, very well organised and beautifully illustrated, will greatly enhance every art lover's journey through the Côte d'Azur.

The French Riviera   Patrick J Murphy

My love affair with the French Riviera in the south of France
began many years ago when I was a schoolboy in Ireland.
Geography was one of my favourite subjects, and I read with
intense interest about this exotic coastal strip of sun-drenched land
by the Mediterranean Sea. This exquisite region, set between the
Alpes-Maritimes and the Alpine Caves, stretches from stately
hillside Menton beside the border with Italy, through the ancient
cities of Nice and Antibes to the more modern city of Cannes,
and ends with the fashionable and fabulous St-Tropez. As a boy,
I believed the French Riviera was exclusively the resort of
millionaires, assorted royalty and gorgeous film stars, and way
beyond the means of ordinary mortals. It took me many years to
discover that it was not only the preserve of the rich but was also
a very accessible destination for ordinary people of moderate means.

I also learned that the French Riviera boasted another unrivalled
attraction in great abundance: antique and modern art of high
quality which is there to be enjoyed by residents and visitors alike.
It may surprise some to learn that there are more than fifty
important art museums and more than 200 other opportunities for
viewing art throughout the Riviera, taking into account ancient and
modern churches, commercial art galleries and public sculptures.
In addition, the region contains some of the grandest belle époque
architecture in the world, and that adds greatly to its attraction for
visiting lovers of the arts.

My first experience of this most beautiful and fascinating corner
of the world was some forty-five years ago when I attended
a convention for maltsters and brewers in Cannes, attended by
delegates from all over the world. I flew into Nice airport with a
colleague and marvelled at the varied and exquisite scenery as we
travelled down to Cannes by taxi. Much fine viewing and dining
took place there in the course of a few days of business before it
was time to return home.

Being a lover and collector of the arts from childhood, I was aware that there was a modern Marc Chagall Museum in the vicinity of Nice, displaying biblical paintings which the artist had bequeathed to the French nation in return for citizenship and patronage. I decided to make a detour and visit the museum for an hour before my departure. It was an unforgettable and enthusing experience to view the gorgeous, modern, colourful paintings and exquisite stained-glass windows of the twentieth-century master, and I resolved to return with my wife and explore more of the wonderful art of the French Riviera. The business colleague who accompanied me on that first occasion declined to enter the museum because he was not interested in art; amazingly, he sat outside instead and read the *Financial Times*, with his back to the heavenly blue Chagall windows through which the sunlight streamed. I don't think he ever realised what a beautiful experience he had missed.

Some years later I was pleased to serve on the judging panel for the annual International Exhibition of Painting held in the Grimaldi Castle at Cagnes-sur-Mer, on the nomination of the Irish Department of Foreign Affairs. Contemporary paintings had been submitted by many countries, including Ireland. My visit was made even more memorable when the seven judges awarded the Palette d'Or, the second most important prize, to the young Irish artist Richard Gorman, who was present for the festivities. He went on to establish an international reputation, and his unique, colourful, abstract forms were recently featured on silk scarves and decorated contemporary designs by the prestigious French couturier Hermès of Paris.

My malt-exporting career took me to many countries throughout Asia, South America, Africa, and of course Europe, where I always managed to visit art galleries in my free time.

Yet nowhere struck me as more beautiful or interesting than
the French Riviera. Rio de Janeiro was stunning and exotic, but
dangerous. The Beach of Passionate Love in Terengganu, Malaysia
was remote and lovely but a bit too hot for pale-skinned Irish
people like me. Mombasa in east Africa offered warm swimming
and access to wildlife safaris, but it was difficult to get to and very
hot. Eventually my wife and I decided to buy a bolthole retirement
apartment somewhere in the French Riviera, with its near-perfect
climate and regular access from Dublin. We holidayed in lovely
Juan-les-Pins one year and spent our afternoons being ferried by
car around the Riviera looking for a residence to suit us. In the end
we decided on Nice, mainly because of its abundance of art riches,
but also because it is the ideal base from which to investigate the
equally rich artistic hinterland. Nice has served the same purpose
for this guide to the French Riviera, through which I hope readers
will be pleasantly escorted around the region to discover the many
wonders awaiting them there – from open air museums in bustling
cities to hidden gems in the remotest of hilltop villages.

Many useful guides have been published about art galleries and
museums in the area, with information on how and when one
might visit them. Tourist offices are also prolific along the French
Riviera, providing all manner of information on opening hours and
bus routes. Indeed, I would have been lost in my endeavours of
artistic exploration without these invaluable aids. With so much
practical information available, *An Art Lover's Guide to the French
Riviera* offers a slightly different approach. My aim in writing this
book is to give readers an insight into the range of possibilities
along the coast, and I hope my commentaries will be of use to some
of the many millions of tourists who visit the French Riviera each
year. Readers of this book will hopefully pick and choose from the
hundreds of options available and use their time most fruitfully.

Obviously, all of the locations dealt with cannot be visited in a short space of time, but some can be set aside for future visits. Regardless of whether readers choose one venue or several, exposure to it has to be life-enhancing, as the connoisseur art dealer Bernard Berenson said. I have certainly found it to be so.

Though I have a lifetime of involvement with the visual arts in Ireland and elsewhere, I have no particular expertise in architecture, local history or Riviera happenings. But I comment on some aspects that appeal to me or seem to be of special interest. I regret that my knowledge of the French language is not better, as it would give me even better insights into the culture of the region. But do not be put off the Riviera if you are not fluent in French. Many natives speak a smattering of English and are fluent in Italian, and they are generally most helpful and polite if the visitor makes even the smallest attempt to speak to them in their own language.

The magic of the French Riviera is hard to define. It comes from the sun glistening off pristine snow on the high Alpes-Maritimes under a canopy of blue sky, from the scent of flowers and shrubs musky in the gentle heat by the coast, and from the perfume of pine trees and olive groves. Orderly rows of fruitful vines border old towns with busy markets, and the bustle of sound from towns and villages lends vibrancy to this idyllic place. Art is but one dimension, but a most important one which has been sewn into the fabric of the Riviera for hundreds of years.

It is no coincidence that this region has attracted some of history's most celebrated artists, composers, philosophers and writers to visit and dwell here. We are now privileged to be able to follow in their footsteps and to enjoy the fruits of their artistic genius.

Ideally the starting point for art exploration is Nice, a handsome
city of some 350,000 people with its modern airport jutting out on a
headland into the cobalt-blue Mediterranean Sea. Most international
flights for the Riviera land here. There is an excellent bus, tram and rail
service throughout the Riviera, as well as frequent taxis, though these
tend to be more expensive than elsewhere. The number 98 bus, which
transports most airport visitors to the city centre, traverses the long
promenade des Anglais which borders the beautiful, sweeping Bay
of Angels (Baie des Anges). It stops a number of times en route,
including outside the magnificent 5-star **Negresco Hotel** with its
wonderful collection of antique and modern art. Residents are
privileged to be able to enjoy this venue, but visitors may also dine
there for morning coffee, lunch at the elegant
La Rotonde restaurant, or afternoon tea in the
café-bar, and also have the pleasure of viewing
the art. The Michelin-starred Chantecler
restaurant is expensive for dinner but well
worth visiting for a special occasion. Its owner,
Madame Jeanne Augier, lives on the top floor
and has willed the hotel to a foundation to
ensure its continuance for posterity.

Negresco Hotel

The Negresco Hotel was built in 1912 by Édouard Niermans for the
Romanian Henri Negresco. A belle époque masterpiece, it became
a listed historic building in 2003 and recently underwent complete
refurbishment. It functions as both a luxury hotel and a spectacular
museum of art. French art is well represented throughout the spacious
building, from the period of King Louis XIII to modern times, though
some of the contemporary works are of lesser quality and interest than
the old masters. Highlights include a splendid full-length portrait of
King Louis XIV, *Sun King*, by the portrait painter Hyacinthe Rigaud
(1659–1743), and a smaller self-portrait in the opposite corner. The
large elegant space of the Salon Versailles also contains a massive stone
chimneypiece taken from a seventeenth-century château. In the
spacious entrance hall leading to the massive Grand Salon oval sitting

area, there is a most attractive bronze bust of portly Madame Renoir by her husband, Pierre-Auguste Renoir (1842–1919). Niki de Saint Phalle's eye-catching multicoloured mixed media sculpture of Miles Davis *The Trumpeter* (1999) stands prominently outside the entrance.

The corridor encircling the oval room, or Salon Royale, is full of modern paintings and sculptures. There is a fine, larger-than-life bronze figure of a young woman by the German sculptor Wilhelm Lehmbruck (1881–1919), an attractive self-portrait by the important painter Madame Louise Vigée-Lebrun (1755–1842), and two striking portrait busts in bronze of the Emperor and Empress of Russia by Oleg Abazieff, made towards the end of the nineteenth century. The Empress, Maria Feodorovna, founded the magnificent Russian Cathedral near the railway station in Nice – an extraordinary piece of architecture that is not to be missed. Completing the outer circle of the Negresco Salon Royale is a very large canvas full of colour and gaiety, titled *Poésie Légère* 1912, by Marie-Félix Hippolyte-Lucas (1854–1925). It may not rank as highly as some of the earlier paintings, but nevertheless it brings a note of elegance and fluidity to the huge, light-filled room with its great Baccarat crystal glass chandelier suspended from the glass ceiling. Beneath it is a glorious Aubusson carpet.

The great inner oval room, with the breathtaking art deco decorated glass ceiling, is flanked by important portraits of French royalty by Jean-Marc Nattier (1685–1766) and Jean-Baptiste van Loo (1684–1745). A complete contrast to these classical works is *La Nana Jaune*, an enormous, bulky, brightly painted and fun sculpture of a young woman, or perhaps fertility goddess, created by modern artist Niki de Saint Phalle (1930–2002) in 1995. The three-metre-high Nana is made from polyester, her body is gaudily painted canary yellow, and she wears a blue swimsuit decorated in bright colours with the sun, moon and stars. Her two great covered breasts are multi-coloured,

Entrance to
the Negresco
Hotel

with a shining sun at the centre of her left breast
and a red heart at the centre of the right. The
swimsuit also has images of a snake, a moon, a
painted hand, red lips and flowers. The figure dances
for joy on one leg, signifying fun and lack of
inhibition on the French Riviera, where the artist
spent much of her working life before dying in the
USA in 2002. The sculpture is mounted on a black
circular plinth which is powered to sometimes rotate
slowly to the strains of piped classical music. The dancing Nana is the
main feature of that grand tranquil space, and it can even be seen from
a distance by passers-by through the entrance door and the long
corridor. You might be inclined to think that this great fat bouncing
lady was something of a self-portrait of the artist, but nothing could
be further from the truth. Photographs of her in the Museum of
Modern and Contemporary Art reveal that she was a very slim woman
into her senior years. In 1949, aged 19 years, she was the cover girl
on *Life Magazine*, modelling haute couture garments captioned
'How to make two outfits out of one'. She and her Swiss-born
sculptor husband Jean Tinguely (1925–91) first came to international
prominence in art when they engaged in shooting at cans of paint
with a rifle to create spectacular paint splashes or explosions. This
planned 'happening' took place in 1961 on waste ground behind Niki
de Saint Phalle's art studio in Paris in front of invited guests: art critic
Pierre Restany, artist Daniel Spoerri, Galerie J director Jeannine de
Goldschmidt, and the unnamed owner of the .22 rifle.

Beside the Negresco Hotel is the most impressive **Masséna Museum**,
another must on my list of places to visit. It is a magnificent piece of
nineteenth-century architecture and is a listed building on the
Historic Monuments inventory. The Villa Masséna
was built in 1898–1901 by the Danish architect
Hans-Georg Tersling (1857–1920) for a member
of the Masséna family. More recently it was donated
to the nation by another member of that illustrious
family. It was subsequently refurbished and re-opened
to the public in 2008 as the museum that presents the
history of Nice in the nineteenth century.

Masséna Museum

It is situated in the midst of a stunning large rose garden, facing onto the rue de France and backing onto the promenade des Anglais through a vista of blue-green sea framed by tall palm trees.

The Masséna Museum is an architectural jewel, with impressive internal marble columns on the ground floor and a very ornate painted ceiling in the huge Portrait Salon. The portraits are of generals and royalty, and are fine but not exceptional artistically; likewise the two large nineteenth-century battle scenes. Upstairs there is an oil portrait dated 1796 of the first André Masséna, who was born to a wine merchant in Nice in 1758, joined the army and was elevated to be a Marshal of France by Napoleon for success in battles before Waterloo. He went on to become Prince d'Essling in 1810 before dying seven years later in Paris. This oil portrait reveals a weak-looking young man magnificently caparisoned, though the carved likeness of him in the rose garden outside portrays a much more determined and forceful-looking individual, who must have been a born leader of men.

Other rooms on the first floor have paintings and prints of Nice and its environs, showing its gradual development from a traditional fishing port with occasional fine buildings, to a splendid, imposing new city of architectural distinction in the days of the influx of rich British holiday-makers escaping their cold wet winters of home. In one room hangs a copy of the famous poster *L'Hiver à Nice*, 1891, by the painter Jules Cheret (1836–1932), and in another a full-length oil portrait, 1885, of the English Queen Victoria (1819–1901) by the artist Heinrich von Angeli (1840–1925).

Portraits of army officers and mayors of the city of Nice appear to have been gathered in from outlying regions to help furnish this gem of a building. This gives visitors a good insight into the cultural history of the region.

General Masséna at the Battle of Essling 1869 Albert-Ernest Carrier-Belleuse Bronze

The most outstanding art museum in Nice is the **Museum of Modern and Contemporary Art (Musée d'Art Moderne et d'Art Contemporain, or MAMAC**). The city contains two other important museums honouring two very great artists, Henri Matisse (1869–1954) and Marc Chagall (1887–1985), but MAMAC is bigger than either and contains a larger, more diverse collection, albeit of more recent vintage. MAMAC is an impressive new building which opened on 21 June, 1990. It is flanked by the National Theatre on one side and the massive Louis Nucéra public library on the other. The modern complex of buildings is in sharp contrast to the older belle époque buildings of the city which are part of its particular attraction. Some commentators describe the new buildings as brash and ugly, but they complement the old and bring a new dimension to the elegant city centre, now that the authorities have demolished the former low-rise bus station and replaced it with the beautiful new promenade du Paillon, which connects MAMAC with the Théâtre de Verdure and runs all the way down to the bay. The new park has fountains and sculptures and, of course, the ubiquitous pollarded ancient olive trees beside new playgrounds, walkways and public toilets.

Steep steps lead up to the spacious forecourt serving the museum and the theatre. Pride of place is given here to two large sculptures by important modern artists, Niki de Saint Phalle (1930–2002) and Alexander Calder (1898–1976). Both were born elsewhere but spent much time working in the French Riviera. The first sculpture is a massive *Loch Ness Monster*, visualised and created by de Saint Phalle from plaster and a mosaic of mirror fragments and paint.

Dollar Sign 1981 Andy Warhol Serigraph and silkscreen

17

The monster has numerous protruding black horns, a long silver tail, and a fearsome golden mouth out of which water trickles into a watery basin, reminding us of the Scottish loch from which the legend originates. It is a most witty piece of modern sculpture that is much photographed by visitors and particularly loved by children. It was generously donated to the museum by the artist in 2001. MAMAC was the eventual recipient of more than 200 of de Saint Phalle's funky, painted assemblages.

The second major sculpture on the MAMAC forecourt is the impressive *Théâtre de Nice* of 1970 by American artist Alexander Calder, fabricated from steel painted black with the moving apex painted red, blue and yellow. Born in Philadelphia, Calder forsook an engineering profession for painting and sculpting and travelled to France in 1926 to become a full-time artist. He first became famous there for exhibiting his miniature fabricated metal circus, and later worldwide for his ingenious *Mobiles and Stabiles*. He was also a regular maker of original prints in bright colours and geometric forms. Young people regularly practise juggling, tango and breakdancing in the vicinity of these two sculptures which stand facing the entrance to the museum and the café beside it.

Théâtre de Nice 1970 Alexander Calder Painted fabricated steel

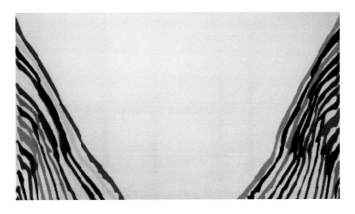

Nearby are two other sculptures which are less conspicuous and of lesser interest: *Scarab* made of metal and wood by Croatian artist Dalibor Stošić (*b.* 1958), and a whimsical see-through *Drape* in white marble by local artist Alexandre Joseph Sosnowsky, popularly known as Sacha Sosno (1937–2013).

The MAMAC building itself is also innovative, consisting of four concrete towers lined by steel and glass walkways. The inner courtyard contains four large permanent art installations commissioned by the city of Nice. One is a typical *Wall Drawing* by American artist Sol LeWitt (1928–2007); the next is *Repetition* by local artist Claude Viallat (*b.*1936); the third is a gigantic assemblage of promenade des Anglais blue chairs by local-born artist Arman (1928–2005); and the final one is a modernistic pop art variation of Manet's famous painting *Déjeuner sur l'Herbe* by French artist Alain Jacquet (1939–2008).

MAMAC has built up an admirable collection of more than 1,400 paintings and sculptures by French and top international artists from the 1950s to the present time. All of the major École de Nice artists are included, and there is also an important group of modern Americans and a growing collection of contemporary British artists, including Richard Long and David Tremlett. The credit for this is due to the expertise and good judgement of its former director from Lille, Gilbert Perlein, who assembled the collection from judicious exhibitions and enticed

Inside the museum entrance is a well-stocked shop selling postcards and souvenirs, and to the right is a small exhibition space where new avant-garde work is regularly displayed. Entry is free on the first Sunday of every month, and at other times the €10 charge is reasonable and worth paying. The museum is closed on Mondays.

donations until 2014, when he had to retire prematurely following an unfortunate accident. American artists include Morris Louis, Robert Rauschenberg, Donald Judd, Andy Warhol, Barbara Kruger, Richard Serra, Tom Wesselman, Claes Oldenburg and Robert Longo. The large acrylic on canvas by the eminent Morris Louis (1912–1962) titled *Alpha Lambda*, 1961, from the *Unfurled* series, is a real treasure. Not many of his works are to be seen outside of the United States. Louis succeeded Jackson Pollock in abandoning paintbrushes to make his paintings by different means. Pollock dripped his paint from cans onto canvases on the floor and became known as Jack the Dripper. Louis leaves the centres of his large canvases bare, but pours successive bands of different colours down the sides of the white canvases in diagonal directions to create rainbow-like effects of abstract painting. He was a direct successor of the American Abstract Expressionists that included leading exponents Robert Motherwell, Franz Kline, Barnett Newman, Clifford Still and others.

The first floor tends to be given over to temporary exhibitions. For me, the most memorable one was of the Chinese artist Cai Guo-Qiang (*b.*1957) in 2010, titled *Travels in the Mediterranean*, when the artist gave a performance with lighted gunpowder, to create amazing images, helped by a team of skilled assistants. He also created a kidney-shaped pool of olive oil flanked by lightning-quick sketches of Nicean bathers and palm trees glimpsed on his quick visit to the Riviera, as well as exhibiting an ancient, wrecked Chinese junk rescued from the seabed, still laden with its cargo of damaged porcelain destined for the European market.

Another floor prominently features works by local School of Nice artists that include Yves Klein, Arman, Sosno, Ben, Niki de Saint Phalle and others. Klein is probably the best known of these internationally, but he died tragically young at thirty-four after a series of heart attacks. Many of his brilliant monochrome paintings and sculptures are here on display. Together with a chemist he invented a special shade of intense Mediterranean blue, known as International Klein Blue (IKB), which was his trademark colour. He is also represented in MAMAC by two eye-catching blue sculptures, his *Blue Victory of Samothrace* and the ethereal *Vénus Bleue*.

Vénus Bleue 1960 Yves Klein Painted plaster cast

In a corridor you will see a tantalising photo-montage of the young Klein diving out of a high window, with outstretched hands, head first onto a seemingly hard pavement several metres below. It is, of course, a trick photograph and an illusion: the artist was in fact diving onto soft tarpaulin held by his artist friends, and the reality was morphed out of the final image. His early death was a sad loss to avant-garde French art. Today his works of art sell on the international market for millions of euro. Visitors to MAMAC should not neglect to proceed upstairs to the roof, where they will pass abstract wall paintings by British artist David Tremlett (*b*. 1945) and encounter other artworks along an exciting walkway that connects the tops of the four towers. From this aerial vantage point there are unrivalled seagulls' views of the most handsome ancient and modern city of Nice, with its Italianate bell towers and gleaming tiled cupolas. One side offers magnificent vistas of the Maritime Alps, another the Bay of Angels. It is quite safe for all except those who may suffer from vertigo, in which case they would be better off proceeding downstairs to the sun-drenched café on the forecourt and enjoying an espresso or Americano in tranquility, while the intrepid sky-walkers are sightseeing overhead.

There are two smaller exhibition spaces facing the promenade des Anglais and the sea which lovers of modern and contemporary art

Ligne Indéterminée 1983 Bernar Venet Black painted steel

should also visit. The first is **Galerie des Ponchettes**, an offshoot of MAMAC that shows items from the permanent collection not always on view at MAMAC itself. It only takes a few minutes to walk about the ancient space, but it is invariably worthwhile. Outside on a large plinth is a striking abstract sculpture in curving black steel by famous local artist Bernar Venet

Arc 11505 1988
Bernar Venet
Black painted steel

(*b.* 1941), titled *Ligne Indéterminée*. Venet seems to be the favourite local artist for public commissions: a giant rusty steel sculpture of nine vertical columns joined at the apex entitled *Neuf Lignes Obliques* was installed in 2010 in front of the Petit Maison restaurant, and the same artist's impressive and enormous *Arc 11505* in black painted steel, dated 1988, is in the nearby public park. Venet has a large studio in Hungary for major fabrications, and has established his own foundation in the Var region at Le Muy.

The second small exhibition space in this vicinity is the **Galerie de la Marine**, which could easily go unnoticed by visitors. It is on the quai des États-Unis near the cours Saleya flower market, perhaps fifty metres further down towards the château from Galerie des Ponchettes. Again it is only a small room in a single-storey building, but it is dedicated to showing contemporary avant-garde work and is worth a quick visit. Each year it features young, prize winning artists from the Villa Arson art college of Nice. It also occasionally exhibits innovative work by visiting international artists. A walking tour of the **Old Town** of Nice (**le Vieux-Nice**) is essential to capture the atmosphere and to enjoy the narrow streets and the many fascinating shops, churches, ateliers, and restaurants. You may make interesting discoveries. On rue Sainte-Réparate there is the Atelier Rifaldi gallery with older art

Neuf Lignes Obliques 2010 Bernar Venet Rusted steel

23

on display behind a large plate glass window. They specialise in the sale and restoration of art and the gallery is well worth a visit – don't be afraid to push in the door and enter. The small space is crowded with minor Impressionist and other more academic paintings, modern prints, drawings, and some examples of African sculpture. The prices are surprisingly modest, and a collector could come away with a lithograph by Picasso for c.€3,000, or a drawing by Yves Klein for a much smaller sum. Not every work of art on the Riviera costs a fortune.

Madame Laure Matarasso of the **Librarie-Galerie Matarasso** in the Carre d'Or centre of the city is also worth a quick visit for admirers of artists' prints and drawings as well as art books. She displays attractive contemporary prints by local artists, and also stocks drawings by modern masters such as André Derain, Paul Jenkins and Léon Zack.

Not too far from there is reputedly the best commercial gallery for modern art in Nice: the **Sapone Galerie** on boulevard Victor Hugo, near the Presbyterian and Lutheran churches. M. Sapone, the father of the present proprietor, was a tailor who made suits for Picasso. He got to know about art through that relationship, and began to deal. The Galerie only opens by appointment. You could expect to see good paintings there by Vivien Isnard, Bernar Venet, Alberto Magnelli, Claude Viallat and other prominent living artists of the region, and you may even discover a work on paper by Picasso or Matisse tucked away in a drawer in the downstairs gallery if you talk nicely to the affable M. Sapone.

The next important excursion is to the hilly suburb of **Cimiez**, where the trees grow very tall. Here you will see art by Matisse and Chagall, both revered modern masters, but you may also discover a local old master of the fifteenth and sixteenth centuries by the name of Ludovico or Louis Brea. More on that anon.

The **Matisse Museum** in Cimiez is a must-see destination in Nice for culture-vultures, though I have some reservations which I will return to later. It is possible to walk all the way up the hill along boulevard Cimiez to the museum if you are youngish and fit and have lots of time to spend, and I have done it, but I recommend that you take the easy way out and step on the number 15 bus beside the Galerie Lafayette department store in place Masséna, and it will get you there in ten minutes. Along the way you will see some outstanding examples of nineteenth-century architecture, most notably the magnificent, dazzling-white Chamber of Commerce building crowned with a sculptural frieze, near the Pastorelli bus stop. Further on you may notice the **Espace Soardi** commercial art gallery, which shows contemporary paintings and photography and which also has a quality picture-framing department. It used to occupy a gallery space on rue Désiré Niel beside the Lycée Masséna, where Matisse set up studio in 1930 to plan and paint the great *Dance* series of canvases for Dr Barnes in Merion, USA. This commission was of such a scale that the artist could not carry it out in his previous studio, so he rented the vacant garage space at number 8 and completed two versions of his favourite theme there before delivering number II to Merion in 1932. Matisse was passionate about women and dancing. To achieve the scale he had to stand on a table and use a long stick with a charcoal tip to initially sketch out the dancing female forms on the three large canvases propped up against the walls. Only then could he begin to paint them in grey against a blue, pink and black background. They are among his greatest achievements, and prepared him to paint the walls of the Rosary Chapel in Vence years later.

Le Vieux-Nice

As you proceed up the hill of Cimiez on the bus, just before the **Matisse Museum** you will see signs for the **Archaeological Museum and Roman Excavations of Cemenelum**. This is worth a quick detour for inquisitive types like myself. The museum houses Roman glass, bronze helmets, small bronzes, lots of ceramic pots and amphorae, sarcophagi and funereal monuments, and other items from the time of Roman occupation. My pick of the exhibits is the larger-than-life marble statue of the haughty Antonia Minor. The excavations themselves are very interesting and reveal how methodical and thorough the Roman invaders were. They had baths with running hot and cold water, and part of the sleeping accommodation still stands. The Arena nearby has been expertly conserved and is said to have seated 4,000 people in its heyday. As you walk through the large olive grove behind the Roman Arena, you will see the lovely red and ochre seventeenth-century Genoese Villa which is now the Matisse Museum, set up as such in 1963 after the artist's death, and extended and modernised in 1993 without taking from its handsome appearance. Apparently, Matisse never lived in the house but was very familiar with it, since he lived just across the road in an apartment in the Hotel Regina, where he also had his studio. When still able to do so, he must often have taken time off to stroll in the olive grove and gaze at the crumbling and partly excavated remains of the great Roman settlement of Cemenelum.

Henri Matisse (1869–1954) was born in the north of France and only arrived to live permanently in the French Riviera in 1918 on the advice of his doctor, who said the sunshine and heat would help cure his bronchitis. He was undoubtedly one of the greatest artists of the twentieth century, vying with his friend and rival Pablo Picasso (1881–1973) for the title of the greatest. The Matisse Museum, alas, does not house the master's most important works which are in museums and private collections worldwide, and so Matisse devotees may feel a little disappointed at the collection on view. But there are some gems here – particularly of his black and white simplified drawings and etchings, of which he was a great master, refining and eliminating detail until he arrived at what he considered to be the absolute essence of the faces and figures before him. He drew and painted his wife and many beautiful models, none more sympathetic to him than the young Russian Lydia Delectorskaya, who was both model and companion to him in his old age. She eventually came between him and his wife, though there is no clear evidence that they enjoyed a sexual relationship. Matisse made many beautiful ink portraits of Delectorskaya, and she was his chief assistant in his later life when he created the enormous paper cut-out compositions in the Regina Hotel apartments, of which *Flowers and Fruit* of 1952 is a fine example and is on permanent view at the museum.

The Cimiez collection is also of interest because it contains a selection of Matisse's small early conventional paintings when he was poor and relatively unknown. *Still Life with Books*, 1890, is a mere 21.5 × 27 cm.

A much larger *Still Life*, dated 1893, is a study after the Dutch/
Flemish master Davidsz de Heem, though in this painting we see
Matisse's love of colour and flair for innovation beginning to emerge.
The Fauve Portrait of *Madame Matisse*, dated 1905, looks to be an
unfinished sketch, though the artist has signed his initials in the
lower right corner. It is a dramatic head-and-shoulders study of a
good-looking young woman with her hair piled up over her head in
the shape of a turban. Her outlines are drawn in black and her face
appears to have been painted rapidly in patches of ochre and red. An
aureole of green paint surrounds the head. The remainder of the canvas
looks raw, but this is deceptive: on close inspection it is actually

painted in a flat beige uniform colour to high-light the portrait. It is a dynamic, experimental, breakthrough painting that seems to anticipate the glorious, expressive, wild paintings of 1912 when Matisse visited Morocco and painted much larger canvases in the vein of *The Standing Riffian* and *The Seated Riffian* with exuberant splashes and patches of bright colour. The young tribesman who was the model has a green cheek and a pink cheek and the painting is intense, immediate and most vibrant.

Another gem in the Cimiez museum is the small oil portrait on board, titled *Tête de Laurette, Fond Vert* 1916. It was painted in Paris. The young sitter has jet black hair and dark eyes, and wears a black dress which is only partly visible. She has a slight twist to one side of her mouth as if to show that she is a reluctant sitter. The background is painted a bright green. It is a powerful, accomplished painting in which Matisse shows that he has arrived at mastery at a young age.

The museum has most of Matisse's important sculptures. He made four massive modellings of the female back in the twenty years between 1909 and 1929, completing *Back IV* in Nice. The first one was quite realistic. The model was a nude woman with a pigtail and her left arm was raised to her head. Later versions became increasingly simplified, and the final version is almost a complete abstraction, with the anatomy reduced to a few vertical lines. All four were cast in bronze in a small edition, and two are on view in the front entrance of the Matisse Museum in Cimiez. I had the luck to see all four at the Hallward Gallery in London in 1967, lent by the Tate Gallery for a fascinating and brilliant Matisse Retrospective Exhibition.

The Matisse Museum has a well-stocked shop upstairs, selling books, souvenirs and postcards. Glass and ceramic items and furniture which belonged to the artist are often on display in the museum and are interesting to see. They do not make up for the dearth of first-class works of art by the artist, but I still return regularly to the museum.

Nature morte aux grenades 1947 Henri Matisse Oil on canvas

After visiting the museum, take time out in the well-tended grey olive grove and enjoy a coffee and a slice of pissaladière: a traditional savoury with onions, olives and anchovies. It is so relaxing to sit in the shade of the unpruned pine trees and watch the mothers and young children enjoying the merry-go-round, or the old men playing boules nearby. In bright sunshine the park exudes great calm and peace, except for the occasional barking of dogs or the cooing of doves. It is now time to move on to the next venue, the beautiful old Franciscan Church just beyond the olive grove.

The **Franciscan Museum**, attached to the singular, beautiful fifteenth-century church and monastery at Cimiez, is often missed by visitors to the nearby Matisse Museum because the complex is not visible from the Matisse Museum in the ancient olive grove. But enthusiasts should persist. It is hidden behind the trees and can be reached by walking a few minutes through the carefully maintained olive trees and mounting a short flight of steps, atop which rests a bronze bust of the recently sainted Pope John Paul II. An impressive stone seraphic cross stands in front of the church.

The church itself is the art treasure, with its five sharply pointed spires and frescoed ceiling. On past visits I have especially enjoyed viewing three masterpieces of religious painting by the famous Nice artist Ludovico Brea (*c.* 1450–1523) and some other paintings by unknown artists. However, the three Brea works were removed in 2014 for conservation and eventual restoration to their original placings. The earliest is the lovely three-panel *Pietà* of 1475 showing Mary grieving over the dead Christ draped across her knees, beneath the cross, while a nobleman on a white horse confers with a soldier in the left-hand panel. In the right-hand panel, a saint in a red cloak holds a shield with one hand and a lance and prayer book in the other. The *Crucifixion* carries the later date of 1512 and is an elaborate composition of great pathos showing haloed disciples of the crucified Christ grieving beneath the cross against a pale blue sky with scudding white clouds. Two noblemen watch nearby. Small panels about the elaborate frame depict bishops and saints, and at the base are fine miniature painted scenes from the taunting and flagellation of Christ. The third and final work by Brea is *Deposition from the Cross*, dated *c*.1515–20. Weeping disciples and relatives with golden haloes and colourful garments attend to the dead Christ, watched by two elderly grieving men at the sides, with a view of Calvary and the three bare crosses in the background. Ludovico Brea came from a creative family, he had an artist brother, Antoine, and a nephew, François, who was a painter.

The church dates from the fifteenth century when the Franciscans came to reside there in the monastery, but it was heavily restored in the nineteenth century. Its stained-glass windows are attractive though not very distinguished, but the altar is most elaborate, with a blue and gold Madonna and Child statue as its centrepiece, flanked by seven-teenth-century sculptures of saints Francis and Dominic.

Visitors may be forgiven for skipping a visit to the cloister, which contains religious paintings that have weathered and are of no great artistic merit, and also for not visiting the top floor Franciscan Museum itself, which contains no great treasures. Yet I feel it is worth the trudge up the flights of steps to see the many simple artefacts that document the Franciscan settlement over the centuries. The chanting of monks can usually be heard in the background, and it is humbling to enter the reconstructed cell of a poor monk of some centuries ago and behold the hard plank bed and simple few items that were allowed for his welfare. A small shop sells beautiful postcards and accepts modest donations.

The final dividend for visiting the Franciscan complex is the walk afterwards through the monastery **Rose Garden**, which has glorious views of the nearby mountains and the sea. Matisse used to walk here in old age in the 1940s to calm his nerves during the

Second World War. The white observatory stands out on the hill over the Paillon gorge, and tiny yachts can sometimes be seen far out in the distant shimmering sea. The roses are at their peak in May and June, and a further little discovery is the sunken garden at the far end, with its geometric tracery of box hedges and vigorous artichokes. The Fort of Mont Alban on an adjoining hillside, formerly a defensive outpost, is also worthy of a visit for intrepid travellers. It is no longer in use and awaits a new function. The Franciscan museum is open daily (except Sundays and public holidays), from 10 am–12 noon and 3–6 pm.

The **Marc Chagall Museum** on the way down from Cimiez, on avenue Docteur Ménard, is the next port of call if the visitor has sufficient stamina. It is a ten-minute walk down the boulevard de Cimiez, or a bus will get you there more quickly. The Chagall Museum is one of the most important museums in Nice, and is not to be missed. It is a low-level modern museum, designed by André Hermant and built by the State in 1973 to house the impressive Biblical Message paintings donated by the artist. These were a token of his gratitude for becoming a French citizen and enjoying freedom from persecution during his residence in France.

Marc Chagall (1887–1985) was born in Vitebsk, Russia. He studied and exhibited his art in difficult circumstances in his native country before emigrating to Germany, where he was eventually classified as a degenerate artist by the Nazis because of his Jewish ancestry. He fled to New York, like many other artists during the Second World War, when the Nazis occupied Paris. After the war, he returned to France and produced a large volume of work – paintings, stained-glass windows for churches, prints, drawings, and even some pieces of small carved stone sculpture.

For a modest entrance fee (with a reduced rate for children), visitors get the loan of an audio guide – but you need to produce a passport, personal identity card or driving licence to get it.

Chagall was a wonderful colourist and a romantic with a vivid imagination, and each visitor will have his or her own favourites of

31

his work. In the room where his early paintings hang, the *Atelier Intérieur* of 1910 has a Soutine-like intensity of passionate brushwork, and the *Blue Circus* painting of 1950 is similarly striking. The large room displaying the big canvases of biblical interpretations will stop you in your tracks even on subsequent visits. *The Battle of Jacob and the Angel* of 1960–66 has searing shades of blue and green, and the predominantly green *Adam and Eve Expelled from Paradise*, 1961, is equally moving; an angel towers over the lovers being borne away on the back of a red cockerel, the latter perhaps a symbol of fertility. The little room containing five other paintings in the *Song of Songs*

Les quatre premiers jours, la Création du monde Marc Chagall Stained glass

sequence is also most impressive. In number IV the lovers are perched on the back of a horse flying over a crowd in a red landscape. On an outside wall nearby, facing a shallow pool, is a large mosaic by the artist featuring the prophet Elijah, dated 1971.

Visitors must also make sure to visit the Auditorium, which contains two grand pianos for occasional concerts. It also has three wonderful Chagall stained-glass windows of varying sizes, all predominantly blue. One is very figurative, with lots of human and animal forms, while the other two tend more towards abstraction. They are very lovely works of art that resonate afterwards in the memory. What an exceptional imagination the artist had! Chagall's genius came, in his own words, from his hands and his heart. Intense Mediterranean blue was one of his favourite colours, and he employed it in most of his stained-glass windows, which numbered fifty in all, as well as in seven tapestries and seven mosaic walls. The Faculty of Science at the University of Nice owns an impressive large mosaic by Chagall on the theme of Odysseus.

The Marc Chagall Museum is situated in a very nicely laid-out garden, with an outdoor restaurant where a refreshing cup of tea can be had in fine weather as the perfect ending to a memorable visit.

Visitors wishing to buy a piece of Riviera art could do well to look in at **Galerie Ferrero** in the rue de Congrès, beside the Palais de la Méditerranée facing the promenade des Anglais. It is invariably well stocked with sculptures by Arman and limited edition signed prints by Chagall, Miró and Picasso, as well as works in a variety of media by lesser-known local artists. In recent years, the proprietors have also opened up a new exhibition space for contemporary artists next door to the main Galerie.

The **Museum of Asian Arts** on the promenade des Anglais, standing in the artificial lake of Parc Phoenix very near Nice Airport, is worthy of a visit by lovers of Oriental Art. The modern building itself, by the renowned Japanese architect Kenzō Tange (1913–2005), is a thing of beauty, quite apart from the treasures on display within. Kenzō Tange also designed the beautiful 1964 Olympic Games stadium in Tokyo.

Admission to the Museum of Asian Arts is free, and there is a shop which stocks exquisite gift items, such as silk scarves, brooches, ceramics, books on Oriental art, postcards and other items. There is also a section where, for a modest cost, visitors can experience the sophisticated, traditional Japanese tea ceremony conducted by an expert teacher wearing a kimono. The museum contains a permanent collection of art and artefacts from India, south-east Asia, China and Japan from olden times, as well as exceptional contemporary items. It puts on periodic special exhibitions reflecting various Asian cultures and forms of modern artistic expression.

The Museum of Asian Arts can be reached by taking the number 9 or 10 bus at place Grimaldi and alighting at Arenas stop, or by taking the number 200 bus for Cannes and stopping at the airport. The number 9 or 10 bus routes pass two other art museums of note, the **Museum of Fine Arts** (Musée des Beaux-Arts Jules Cheret) followed by the **Anatole Jakovsky International Museum of Naïve Art**. All three museums deserve to be visited, though their footfall is noticeably lighter than in the MAMAC, Matisse and Chagall museums.

A visit to the Museum of Asian Arts is strongly recommended. For a start, it is a stunningly beautiful modern example of architectural art. Kenzō Tange himself has written: 'The Museum is a white jewel that shines beside the Côte d'Azur. It is shaped like a swan floating on the calm waters of a lake close to the Mediterranean, among luxurious vegetation'.

Han dynasty 200 BC - 220 AD *Ceramic horses*

Tange explains that the building is designed on the simple geometric forms of the square and the circle, and makes reference to the oriental concepts of yin and yang.

I particularly like walking through the museum and watching white swans and black swans swim gracefully by, under a little stone bridge which connects the exhibition space with the tea ceremony pavilion. Around the Museum of Asian Arts there are also scores of ducks and geese paddling about in the waters of Le Parc Phoenix, ready to snap up offerings of bread from visitors with their children. Le Parc is well worth a visit in its own right – for its extraordinary collection of flora and fauna, some housed in the immense, brilliantly designed glass and metal greenhouse known as the Green Diamond, and for an exhibition hall at the entrance in which art exhibitions are held from time to time. Le Parc presents temporary exhibitions of sculpture each year, and also has permanent exhibits. The admission fee is only €2, and Le Parc also offers dining facilities.

The Chinese Room of the Museum of Asian Arts is small and contains only a small number of works of art, but they are superb examples. The great bronze Bo Bell stands out, as do the Han dynasty ceramic figures. The Japanese Room has ancient rattan flower baskets for *ikebana* and a pair of elegant Japanese screens that celebrate books and civilisation. The Southeast Asian Room shows stone carvings from Angkor Wat in Cambodia, which is now a World Heritage Cultural phenomenon. A carved white marble sculpture of an Indian Goddess Salabhanjika of voluptuous proportions touching a mango tree is a miracle of tenth-century art from Rajasthan.

Several other works, outstanding of their kind are on permanent display. Of particular note are the gilded bronze kneeling *Buck and Doe*, of fourteenth- or fifteenth-century Tibet, that symbolises the first sermon of the Lord Buddha, and the seated bronze

sculptures from fifteenth-century Nepal of the god *Indra and his wife Indrani*, king and queen of the gods in that region.

The Museum of Asian Arts is a place of infinite calm and serenity. Upstairs, it exhibits ancient ceramics and large sculptures, of which the thirteenth-century Thai standing Buddha is noteworthy. You can experience this little museum in fifteen minutes or an hour, according to your interest and state of mind. Many visitors never seem to get there, which is a great pity, as they are missing something special.

Museum of
Asian Arts

The **Anatole Jakovsky International Museum of Naïve Art**, in the Fabron district, is of lesser interest. Admission is free, but it closes from 12 to 1 pm for lunch, and late arrivals around noon could usefully spend luncheon in the adjoining Parc Carol de Roumanie, where refreshments may be purchased.

Anatole Jakovsky was a writer of Romanian origin who lived in Paris and had a passion for naïve art, much of which he is said to have acquired in the Paris flea market at modest cost. He and his wife Renée eventually donated their collection to the French State, which augmented it and housed it here in what was formerly Château Sainte-Hélène, built in the nineteenth century and modified a few times since. It previously belonged to the perfumier Coty, who sold it to the city of Nice in 1982, when it became this Naïve Museum.

The collection is short on masterpieces, as one might expect, but it does have a portrait of Frumence Biche in formal dress and black tie, by the famous painter, Henri Rousseau, also known as Le Douanier Rousseau, (1844–1910), friend of Picasso and Modigliani. It also has a few good paintings by André Bauchant (1873–1958) of which *A View of Vence from the Ramparts* and *The Harvesters* are memorable. A painting of Ville d'Orsay, 1945, by French artist Jean Eve (1900–68) catches one's eye. An American artist, Gertrude Allen O'Brady (1901–85), obviously knew Jakovsky well, as she painted his portrait at least twice, once lying down smoking his pipe and gazing at the numerous paintings he had collected hanging about him on the walls of his home, and the other a very competent small head-and-shoulders portrait of the writer, dated 1941. There is also a remarkably attractive painting of a dead tree by the American Naïve artist best known as Grandma Moses (1860–1961).

The upstairs gallery is sometimes not open to the public, but a ground-floor room is devoted to paintings from Croatia, and these are interesting and have a certain primitive honesty. Many are examples of reverse glass painting, a process that survives from Greek and Roman antiquity, and a style that was practised by the Chinese for centuries.

The museum is a ten-minute walk up the Fabron Hill from the rue de France. It has a small shop which sells postcards, small souvenirs, etchings and posters.

The **Musée des Beaux-Arts Jules Cheret**, also known as the **Fine Arts Museum**, on avenue des Baumettes is an important museum, well worth visiting for lovers of older art. It is located in a very handsome, ochre and cream, classical nineteenth-century villa approached by a wide arrangement of steps ascending from the rue de France, a mere ten-minute walk from the Negresco Hotel. It was built by a Ukrainian princess and was originally known as Villa Kotchoubey. It was later purchased by a rich American before it acquired its present municipal function. Like the two small museums previously mentioned, it does not attract large crowds, but it is all the more enjoyable for that reason. It inherited works of art from the first Municipal Museum of Nice together with loans from the Louvre in Paris and other regional state museums, and it has been open to the public in its present location since 1928. The works on display range from the thirteenth to the twentieth century and include paintings and sculptures by some big-name artists, such as Bronzino, Rodin, Carpeaux, Fragonard, Delacroix, Corot, Bloemaert, Velvet Brueghel, and moderns such as Bonnard, Dufy, Van Dongen, Kisling, Laurencin, Valtat, Lebasque, and Luce.

Musée des Beaux-Arts Jules Cheret

The first big room has massive allegorical nineteenth-century paintings by local academic artists Van Loo – apparently three artists bore that surname. They have been derided by some critics as being of little interest, but they are worth viewing and are technically impressive. The next room has an impressive tree-filled landscape by Camille Corot (1796–1875), and the round self-portrait, 1769, of an old and seemingly disillusioned Jean-Honoré Fragonard (1732–1806) is satisfyingly revealing.

Some of the masterpieces of this museum are in the next little room; six of the seven oil paintings hanging there were donated by a Madame Aline Avigdor d'Acquaviva in 1995–96. Two undoubted masterpieces are the lovely medium-sized *Allegories of Water and Land*, painted on curved wood panels by Jan (Velvet) Brueghel (1568–1625) and Hendrik von Balen (1575–1632). The first shows a near-naked Venus and attendant infants, surrounded by fish of all kinds and seashells and crabs, with the sea and fantastic figures in the background and a lone male figure at the side. *The Allegory of the Faith* reveals a similar partially naked Venus figure with three attendant infants, or putti, while a reclining Bacchic male figure holds a sheaf of corn amidst a foreground of myriad fruits, vegetables and flowers. In the background there is a castellated hill to the left and a distant view of a church's steeple with reapers of corn in the nearby field. Both panels have been recently cleaned and are a very good addition to the museum. The donor also gave a seventeenth-century Flemish painting of *Christ on the Road to Emmaus*, and a matching painting of women journeying through a mountainous landscape, by Dutch artist Adriaen Van Nieulandt (1587–1658); these complement the previous works, though they are of a lesser standard. Another of her gifts was the large, excellent oil painting *Angélique est Médor* by Abraham Bloemaert (1564–1651), which also appears to have been recently cleaned. In 1978 the museum purchased a fine painting of *David Holding the Head of Goliath* by Hendrik Van Somer (1615–85) to hang beside it. The final gift of excellent taste and good judgement from Madame Aline is a small painting of *David and Abigail* by Frans Francken (1581–1642). It completes the ensemble of that magical small room.

The ground floor has a sculpture court with a number of works, including *Triumph of Flora*, 1873, in plaster, by Jean-Baptiste Carpeaux (1821–75), and a marble carving of *The Three Graces*, after Antonio Canova (1757–1822). Upstairs there are two bronze sculptures by Auguste Rodin (1840–1917) and a plaster cast of his famous carving *The Kiss*.

The Impressionist room of the Fine Arts Museum has an attractive collection of paintings by mostly lesser-known French artists of the nineteenth and twentieth centuries, of which the standout is probably a landscape seen through a window by the major figure Pierre Bonnard.

One complete room is devoted to the paintings and a few ceramics of Raoul Dufy (1877–1953), who frequented the Riviera. A favourite work is the very freely painted *Big Tree of Sainte-Maxime* of 1972, with its great sweep of blue sky overhead. Another small room contains the strange small figurative painting of Nice's father-and-son artists, Alexis and Gustav-Adolf Mossa. Both were well known locally for their fantastic contributions to the annual Carnaval de Nice in the twentieth century. Yet another room is completely given over to the painting of Jules Cheret, after whom the museum is named. Cheret (1836–1932) was a resident of Nice and the belle époque's favourite poster painter. His large oil paintings are full of colour and light, but lacking in gravitas. His star has now waned in the art world, but his large canvas *Le Déjeuner sur l'Herbe* is typical of him at his best, if a far cry from the painting of the same title by the great Édouard Manet.

The upstairs corridor has interesting nineteenth-century academic paintings by Marie Bashkirtseff (1858–84), a Russian princess who painted in Paris and Nice and was friendly with the Irish painter Sarah Purser HRHA (1848–1943). It also contains good examples by the influential teacher Bastien-Lepage (1848–84).

The final masterpiece in this calm and infrequently visited museum, and one worth the visit alone, is the astonishing *Crucifixion*, *c.*1540, in oil on a wood panel by the Italian old master Agnolo Bronzino (1503–72), who worked during the golden age of painting in Florence. The crucified, almost naked Christ hangs nailed to a plain brown cross in the forefront of a grey architectural alcove that is painted in a cold, metallic style for which this artist was noted. There is no other human being in the painting. The icy coldness but brilliant precision of the thinly painted composition is in keeping with the evidence that Christ is alone and has died for the sins of others. I suspect it has been recently cleaned or restored; if the latter, then the work has been carried out flawlessly. One could almost believe it was painted recently, so modern and timeless is the style, if it did not carry its attribution to Bronzino. It is painted in oil, though the surface has an almost metallic or enamelled appearance. The Metropolitan Museum in New York has a portrait of a young man by Bronzino in which he employs the same device of including a grey architectural feature as a background. Both of these paintings are very different from the artist's great masterpiece *Venus, Cupid, Folly and Time* in the collection of the National Gallery in London. This is an erotic allegorical composition in which a young, wonderfully endowed and kneeling Venus dallies with an equally naked adoring little Cupid, while a decrepit old man looks on from the blue background, representing the future and the sadness of old age. The flesh of the naked figure is painted in a similiar icy white.

Sculpture at the Musée des Beaux-Arts, Carnolès, Menton

Bronzino's style was very different from that of his more flamboyant master Correggio (1489–1534), who painted with greater brio. But the pupil was an extraordinarily gifted draughtsman and painter in his own right, tightly controlling his subject matter, as in his great *Crucifixion*, where grey and black are used to strong effect in the background to elicit sympathy and sadness in the viewer. To give the illusion of modernity, the painting is presented in the museum in a clinical plain grey frame. I do urge you to visit the museum and see this painting. Regretfully, the museum authorities have not yet made a postcard of it. It is my increasing experience in art museums that my favourite paintings are often not reproduced. Popularity seems to outweigh excellence.

The **Palais Lascaris** can be found on rue Droite in the Old Town, and visitors to Nice should not miss a visit to this wonderful, aristocratic palace, now converted to a museum. Not only is it filled with many treasures, but it has also been listed as a national historic monument since 1946. The palace was built in 1648–57 for the Count Lascaris-Vintimille, nephew of the 57th Grand Master of the Order of Malta, and it remained the property of that family until the French Revolution. Sold in 1802, it was converted into flats and gradually deteriorated until purchased in 1942 by the city of Nice, which handsomely refurbished it. The style is Genoese baroque, as is the case for many of the finest churches of the period in Nice. The layout is organised around two small interior courtyards, from the vestibule of which winds a magnificent stone and marble staircase, crowned with impressive sculptures of Mars and Venus, accompanied by a number of portrait busts in elegant niches. The arched ceiling in the vestibule is frescoed and bears the coat of arms of the family Lascaris-Vintimille. Inside the entrance door and to the left is a shop which sells souvenirs, postcards and books, though it is not kept well stocked. Outside the shop is a fine bronze portrait bust of Grand Master Jean-Paul Lascaris, dated 2000, by Maltese artist Joseph Chetcuti, after the original by Covati, *c.*1658. On the other side of the ground floor, there used to be a reconstructed pharmacy of 1738 on view, with interesting Delftware pottery, but this has recently been closed off. Perhaps the authorities decided it was not really part of the history of the building in the first place.

The first floor is plain enough, with rooms on either side of the staircase displaying stringed instruments such as violins, mandolins and harps, made in Nice from the nineteenth century to the present day – a proud local tradition. Sometimes the room on the left is used for temporary exhibitions: in 2013 the suite of jazz prints by Matisse were displayed as part of an eight-museum celebration of that artist's life and work, on the occasion of the fiftieth anniversary of the opening of the Matisse Museum in Cimiez.

The second floor is much grander and is beautifully furnished with tapestries, paintings, sculptures, antique musical instruments, fine period furniture and frescoed ceilings. The small, elegant chapel to the right has a large cartouche in the ceiling illustrating *Wisdom Defying Time and Death*. It was painted by a member of the School of Carlone, Genoa in the seventeenth century. Wisdom is personified by the goddess Athena (Minerva), identifiable by her helmet and shield. Next to her is Cronus (Saturn), who was reputed to have eaten his own young and is portrayed as a winged old man holding an hourglass. Also represented is the ouroboros – a serpent biting its own tail – symbolising the perpetual cycle of time and eternity. Dominating the composition is a cherub, the harbinger of death, holding a scythe. The chapel is also decorated with a number of paintings by unknown artists, and one can usually hear background music by Tomaso Albinoni (1671–1751), recorded by the Baroque Ensemble of Nice.

The room outside contains two fine large oil paintings by the Venetian artist Francesco Pittoni (1645–1724). One is titled *The Creation of Adam and Eve*, the other *The Expulsion of Adam and Eve from the Garden of Eden*. More antique musical instruments are displayed here, including a grand piano and a harpsichord, as well as some anonymous portraits. In the adjoining salon of the Knights of the Order of Malta there is a splendid anonymous large painting, in the Lombardy eighteenth-century style, of a voluptuous reclining Mary Magdalene surrounded by cherubs. The remaining small rooms contain some good furniture and small landscape paintings in the manner of Vernet.

The rooms to the left on the ornate second floor are hung with fine large seventeenth-century Aubusson tapestries after Isaac Moillon (1614–73) and Sir Peter Paul Rubens (1577–1640). Off the main

room is a lavishly furnished bedroom with fine furniture and a great blue and white ceramic plate with the Lascaris coat of arms emblazoned on it. The third floor is not open to the public.

Nice's old town is full of interest for visitors on foot. The streets are very narrow, and the rue Droite in particular has many ateliers and art galleries with a variety of items for sale, though the quality may not suit everyone.

The narrow streets of Nice

Flea market at cours Saleya

The same thing might be said about the antiques market held on stalls in the lovely **cours Saleya** every Monday morning. Popularly known as the Nice flea market, it displays all manner of old artefacts, implements, furniture, paintings, prints, ceramics, textiles, pewter and what have you, and everything is for sale. Most things are priced, but bargaining is the norm, and while many items are only of passing interest, there is always the possibility of discovering an unrecognised treasure at a giveaway price. Old master drawings do sometimes turn up, but the buyer must beware. Purchases are for cash, and no guarantees are given. At lunchtime the market closes and the cours Saleya becomes a thronged outdoor dining area. On other mornings of the week it becomes the colourful flower market. Stalls display the wares artistically, and provide ideal material for tourists' photographs.

At the far end of the cours Saleya stands a handsome, tall, yellow and ochre building at **1 place Charles Félix**, where the great artist Henri Matisse lived for seventeen years. The bright marketplace colours and the Mediterranean light enthralled and enthused him to paint many fine pictures that are redolent of that ambiance. So far, there is no plaque on the wall to inform visitors that he lived there, though there is one on the wall of Hôtel Beau Rivage, where he first lived in Nice.

Galerie Lapita, a commercial art gallery on the ground floor of
No. 1 place Charles Félix, specialises in Oceanic sculpture and Australian
Aboriginal paintings. It has many good examples in stock, on view and
on sale, and purchases can be shipped worldwide. It is worth a visit.
As mentioned earlier, le Vieux-Nice, or the Old Town, is full of interest
because of its shops, architecture, historic churches with art, and many
outdoor sculptures. They are too numerous to mention them all, but the
following churches may be of particular interest to readers.

Église St-Martin-St-Augustin is one of the city's oldest parish churches.
It was built in 1144 and has gone through many phases over the intervening
centuries. It still opens for Mass on weekdays and Sundays and is a listed
historic monument. Its treasures include a wonderful *Pietà* painting, *c.* 1500,
attributed to Nice artist Louis Brea. The church was assaulted by the
Turkish army in 1543, and a cross marks the spot where a cannonball burst
through its walls during the siege of the city. Martin Luther celebrated
Mass there on his journey to Rome to remonstrate with the Pope in 1514.
Giuseppe Garibaldi, the unifier of Italy, was also baptised there in 1808.

On the ancient wall opposite the entrance to the church is a relief sculpture
plaque to the memory of local heroine Catherine Ségurane, erected in 1923.
She was a humble laundress who inspired the citizens to take up arms and
defend the city against the Turkish attack in 1543. She is depicted as a
fine-figured young woman holding a washing paddle in one hand and
brandishing a raised flag of defiance in the other. The nearby fish market
at place Saint-François is memorable for its noisy, pungent selling of
fish which takes place every morning except Mondays. In its centre is
an attractive fountain of four dolphins spouting water into the surrounding
marble trough. The dolphins' entwined tails are crowned with a ball and

seem to be carved from some porous volcanic
stone which contrasts sharply with the harder
marble beneath.

Nearby is a grand, decrepit old building from
1580, known as the Palais Communal, which is
soon to be refurbished by the city authorities.
The municipal authorities take a great pride in
their historic heritage.

The tall **Tour de Saint-François**, with its splendid large clock from 1836–41 and bells looking out over the city towards MAMAC, was once part of a Franciscan convent. It is now, thankfully, a preserved historic monument. If you walk down the incline behind it on the rue de la Tour, you will see the dereliction of part of the old wall, and, on the other side of the dark alley, residences and the Théâtre de l'Impasse. Some other churches in the Old Town are well worth visiting. The **Cathédrale Saint-Réparate**, built in the seventeenth century and partially refurbished in 2014, has a splendid tiled dome by architect Jean-André Guibert and an aspect of appropriate gravitas on place Rosetti. The interior is richly decorated in baroque style with seraphim and cherubim in abundance and many fine paintings. It stages an outdoor life-size crib at Christmastime.

Chapelle de la Miséricorde on cours Saleya

The **Église Saint-Jacques Le Majeur** on nearby rue Droite and place du Jésus was built by the Jesuits in 1642–85. It is no longer regularly open to the public, but is correctly designated a historic building and is said to contain works by local painter Hercule Trachel (1820–72). The **Église Notre Dame de l'Annonciation** on the rue de la Poissonnerie, just off the cours Saleya, is another historic building from the seventeenth century and is crammed with fine paintings, sculptures, and a decorated ceiling. It has a special dedication to St Rita.

The focal point of the cours Saleya itself is the **Chapelle de la Miséricorde** of 1740, a small baroque masterpiece, recently restored. It is open only for Mass on Sundays. Its interior is gloriously decorated in gold and stucco, and its sacristy boasts a splendid early Renaissance painting of 1430, Politique de la Miséricorde, by local artist Jean Mirailhet. It was and is patronised by the Black Penitents.

The White Penitents patronise the elegant **Chapelle Sainte-Croix**, with its splendid facades on rue Saint-Joseph, which underwent refurbishment in 2014 at a budget of €1.65 million. The confraternity of White Penitents is said to be the oldest in Nice, dating back to its foundation in 1306. Then there is the fine neoclassical **Chapelle du Saint-Sépulchre** patronised by the Blue Penitents, facing onto the square on place Garibaldi. It was redesigned by the eighteenth-century architect Antoine Spinelli and dates from 1431, when the Franciscans first came to live in the area. It is open to the public in the afternoons, and mass is still celebrated there. It is also a historic baroque building and was restored in 2000. Visitors might almost pass this church

without spotting it up close, since all sides of the lovely arcaded square are now filled with fish restaurants, shops and a cinema. **Garibaldi Square** itself is a protected historic area, with beautiful symmetry and pale colouring, dating from the eighteenth century.

In the centre of the square is the impressive statue of Giuseppe Garibaldi, carved from white marble and elevated on a fine pedestal. The local hero is flanked by two bronze lions and gazed at by two young women crowned with laurels who brandish flags and are minding a baby, all seemingly cast in bronze in 1891. At the base of the monument are smaller carved marble reliefs honouring brothers Constante and Bruno Garibaldi, grandsons of Giuseppe, who both died in 1914 in World War One. At the back, facing towards the church is a fine bronze relief panel of Amazons with flags celebrating victory. The artist's name, carved at the base of the plinth, is Gustave Deloye. He was assisted by Antoine Étex.

The **Église Saint-François-de-Paule**, on avenue de Pessicart, is less grandiose than the previously mentioned ancient heritage buildings. It is still in daily use, frequented by mass-goers. The vaulted ceiling is bare for some reason; war damage in the past may have obliterated fresco paintings. It is the Church of the Dominican Order, and inside there is a fine, possibly twentieth-century wood carving of a full-length

Saint Dominic. The altar is noteworthy for its central crucifixion sculpture, surrounded at back and sides by oil paintings of religious subjects, some of which are said to have been painted by local artist Hercule Trachel. The side chapels have what appear to be nineteenth-century paintings. The church has only plain-glass windows.

Beside the church is **Galerie des Dominicains**, an art exhibition space given over to temporary exhibitions by less well known artists from France and emerging artists from Africa. Works are invariably for sale at modest prices, and some good exhibitions of paintings from Tanzania have recently found ready buyers there. Admission is free, and it is open on most days.

Nice Opera House

Just a short distance from the cours Saleya, **Nice Opera House** is opposite the Dominican church on rue Saint-François-de-Paule. With its ornate façade and glorious belle époque interior, this is one of my favourite buildings in the city. Designed by local architect François Aune, it is a typical nineteenth-century Italianate construction, originally built in 1826 but rebuilt in 1885 after a terrible fire destroyed the building, with severe loss of life. The frescoed ceiling is blistering a little bit nowadays and could do with a makeover, but it still has its aura of grandeur, with a massive glass chandelier and relief sculptures in gold of bare-bosomed angels playing trumpets in tribute to the god of music and to the leading Italian composers of opera. Its outer roof is crowned with a quartet of standing, baroque stone figures, which evidently have withstood the vagaries of climate.

Nice Opera House is also a listed building and stages seasonal programmes of opera, ballet and classical music, well patronised by citizens and tourists alike.

The other church I would recommend for art lovers to visit is the much more recent Anglican **Holy Trinity Church** on rue de la Buffa, in the Carré d'Or near place Grimaldi. It dates from 1820 and was expanded in 1860 in the neo-Gothic style that was fashionable at that time. It was financed by the English-speaking community, who mostly came from Great Britain. In fact, the apse of the church was not completed until 1913. The east windows were only installed after the First World War. These three beautiful stained-glass windows were made in Chartres by the reputable atelier Lorin and are the main reason art lovers should visit. Other stained-glass windows there are by Mayer of Munich, Cottier and Clayton Bell of the United Kingdom, and the north and west windows by Payet and Roy of Lyon.

Burial place of Rev Henry Francis Lyte in the Holy Trinity Church cemetery

The church is open daily, and to see the Mediterranean light streaming through these miraculously coloured windows, against a background of gently piped plain chant, is especially satisfying. At the rear of the church is a small cemetery where the Irish prelate Reverend Henry Francis Lyte (1793-1847) is buried. He was a pastor here who is best remembered for composing popular hymns, of which the most famous is 'Abide With Me'. The church's exterior was cleaned and refurbished in 2012–13 with help from the city of Nice, and it is a distinctive building in the area. Musical events are sometimes staged in the church when services are not in progress. A feature of the external fabric of the building is the number of small carved sandstone heads protruding from the sides of the windows. It is now speculated that they represent images of English kings and queens, including James I, Charles I, and Victoria, and possibly the heads of William Shakespeare, Christopher Marlowe, and other artistic eminences of the past.

A decision by the authorities in Nice to install a tram system to bisect the city and improve rapid communication was a very good idea. Installing the tram-tracks made for disagreeable disruption for some years, but when completed it was a very worthwhile addition to the city. With the completion of Phase 1 of the tramway, one can now traverse Nice from Las Planas to Pont Michel, a distance of 8.7 kilometres, for the modest price of €1.50. Phase 2 of an underground tramline from the port to the airport is now underway.

For Phase 1 the authorities set aside approximately €4.5 million to commission new works of art for the tramline, a small percentage of the total project budget, in line with progressive *Per Cent for Art* policies in some other European countries. The original concept was that one reputable artist would be invited from each European Union country. In the end, the selection by a jury of French art experts was something of a compromise. Thirteen artists were commissioned, one each from Great Britain, Spain and Germany, and ten from France. They obviously set about their tasks with imagination and alacrity, and the result is that Nice can justly claim today to have the largest open air museum of contemporary art in the south of France. It is to be hoped that a similarly enlightened policy will apply to Phase 2.

Thirteen artists were selected to enhance the tramway:

Ben (Benjamin Vautier)
Michael Craig-Martin
Gunda Förster
Yann Kersalé
Ange Leccia
Stéphane Magnin
Jean-Michel Othoniel
Pascal Pinaud
Jaume Plensa
Emmanuel Saulnier
Pierre di Sciullo
Sarkis (Serkis Zabunyan)
Michel Redolfi

The artist Michael Craig-Martin (*b.* 1941) was chosen to represent Great Britain, where he lives, though he was born in Dublin and grew up in the USA, studying art and architecture at Yale University. This was a very good choice for Nice. He is a distinguished avant-garde artist who absorbed the tenets of minimalism and conceptual art before developing his own unique artistic vision that rejects conventional painting and sculpture. Craig-Martin's wall drawings and paintings are among the furthest out from the city centre, but

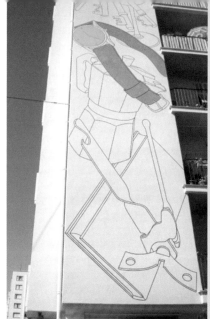

Cascade d'objets 2007 Michael Craig-Martin Acrylic paint

the efficient Veolia tram will take you there, direction Hôpital Pasteur, in ten or fifteen minutes. Along the way you will pass the Vauban bus station, followed by the Université Nice Sophia Antipolis campus, before the tram stops right beside the artist's installations on the end walls of four high-rise apartment blocks. It is my favourite work of the Open Air Museum. You need to get off the tram and walk about boulevard Virgile Barel to fully experience the wit and extent of this thinking artist's accomplishment.

Craig-Martin has drawn in black paint a trademark outline composition of eight modern objects, interestingly juxtaposed on the long narrow vertical panels of each apartment block. The items are a guitar, a running shoe, a glass of liquid, a bunch of keys, a wrist-watch, a coffee percolator, a book, and finally what looks like a long-handled tin and bottle opener. Only one object is painted in colours on each block. Proceeding up the boulevard you first see a purple and orange guitar on black, with the other items in outline only. On block 2 the key ring and keys are in bright yellow, green, purple and blue, and the rest are in outline only. On block 3 only the watch and strap in the middle of the composition are painted in bright colours: blue for the face, gold surround and purple strap. On block 4 the tin and bottle opener at the bottom of the composition is in full colours of blue, orange and red, while the rest are again in outline. The colours follow in descending order. You, the viewer, must then proceed beyond the apartment blocks to rue Francis Carco and turn about and retrace your steps, looking up at the reverse side panels of the four apartment blocks. The artist has here used the same eight objects to make a similar composition but in a different juxtaposition of the objects on the panels. The composite work of art is both thoughtful and ingenious and also rather lovely to look at, among these working-class buildings separated by rows of carefully pollarded plane trees, and in the shadow of a tree-clad hill slope.

The Spanish artist Jaume Plensa (*b.* 1955) got the prime spot on place Masséna in the city centre beside the ochre buildings that include the luxury department store Galerie Lafayette. He is well known on the French Riviera, with a large outdoor public sculpture facing the sea at Antibes, and previous exhibitions at the Picasso Museum in the same town.

Conversation à Nice 2007 Jaume Plensa Stainless steel, polyester resin, fibreglass and LED (1 of 7 figures)

Here in Nice he has created seven seated and crouching human forms, made of polyester resin and fibreglass, that are spaced out along the grand square on twelve-metre-high stainless steel poles. They remind one of Buddha in the lotus position and other poses. Yet Plensa's sculptures are dynamic: they contain electroluminescent diodes which enable them to light up in different colours at night, bringing glamour and atmosphere to that popular rendezvous scene. The artist had in his mind to represent the different continents and the dialogue that constantly takes place between the many communities that inhabit or visit Nice. The title is *Conversation à Nice*.

Yann Kersalé's *L'Amorse du bleu*, an extensive light installation spanning part of boulevard JeanMedécin, can be found a tram-stop further down from place Masséna. It is another highlight of the Open Air commissions. Using the latest technology and steel cables criss-crossing the central boulevard, he has created a wonderland of cobalt blue and emerald-green luminosity that is simply entrancing after nightfall, either from within a passing tram or at a distance from place Masséna.

Another artist to make use of light as her primary material is the German Gunda Förster. Appropriately for Nice, she pays homage to the late Yves Klein by creating two blue installations from fluorescent tubes under railway bridges, and these are visible to observant pedestrians even in normal daylight. The remaining artists chosen were all French, and at least four of them live and work in Nice. Their names are Pierre di Sciullo, Ange Leccia, Stéphane Magnin, Pascal Pinaud, Jean-Michel Othoniel, Michel Redolfi, Emmanuel Saulnier, Ben, and the installation artist Sarkis, who was born in Istanbul but is a long-time resident of France and an international figure. His *False Gate* installation at an entrance to the Old Town is an understated combination of gold leaf and coloured slabs of veined marble that works beautifully, even if it is not recognised as a work of art by many of those who climb the steps and pass through it.

I have walked and travelled by train to view all of the new outdoor works of art and find that they all have their admirable traits, though I have to confess that the sound pieces by Michel Redolfi that can be heard from time to time, apparently on the tram sides, have escaped me, possibly because I am becoming hard of hearing.

All in all, the Open Air museum was a daring adventure and I consider it a resounding success. The few hundred new works of art at the various tram stops, when you take into account artist Ben's iconic calligraphic aphorisms and Pierre di Sciullo's high-tech tram aluminium signs painted in blue and ochre and also mounted on steel poles, really do bring modern art out into the public spaces, and they are none the worse by being so different from the more traditional art of yesteryear to be seen in the indoor museums.

L'Observatoire Astronomique de Nice on the boulevard de l'Observatoire, high up on a hill overlooking Nice, is worthy of a visit by keen explorers. The lovely white main building can be observed from Cimiez and many other parts of the city. The great sliding dome was designed by Gustave Eiffel (of the Eiffel Tower), and the building by Charles Garnier (of the Paris Opera). The massive 59-foot lens was once the largest in the world, and astronomers discovered more than 2,000 stars at this site since its construction. The spacious grounds contain altitude shrubs and flowers, as well as some sculptures. It can be reached by bus, car or on foot.

Cathédrale Orthodoxe Russe St-Nicolas, 1913, better known as the **Russian Orthodox Cathedral**, is located on avenue Nicolas II, boulevard Gambetta, a few blocks from Nice's main railway station. It is well worth a visit: for the beauty of its architecture, including six onion domes, and for the many fine painted frescoes and icons in the interior. It is open daily to the public for a small fee, except during services on Sundays. It underwent restoration in 2015 for the first time since it was built.

The design of the building was based on a five-domed church of Jaroslav near Moscow. It was built in the age of Tsar Nicolas II, 1903–12, before the Russian Revolution, and the very best materials were employed from Italy and the south of France, without stinting on cost. Visitors are expected to be appropriately dressed; shorts and sleeveless shirts are not permitted. There is a small shop which sells postcards and souvenirs. In the park nearby is a morbid Byzantine mortuary chapel of the architect Grimm, where the consumptive young Tsarevich Nicholas was buried in the nineteenth century.

Prieuré des Vieux-Logis can be found on avenue Saint-Barthélemy. This charming old Priory balustrade building of the Order of St Dominic is situated in a small, colourful, unkempt garden with ancient olive trees, palms and an orange tree. The surrounding residences are much more recent. It most notably houses a collection of antique religious art dating from the fifteenth to the sixteenth century, collected by a Dominican monk, A. J. Lemedde, OP. The *Cadogan Guide to the South of France* states that the pride of the collection is a fifteenth-century Flemish Pietà. The old Villa Niçoise was renovated in 1939 and donated by the Order to the city of Nice as a legacy gift. Unfortunately, it is normally padlocked, and a resident from the Avenue informed this writer that there is only one day in the year, in October, when neighbours can visit it. However, the tourist guide does state that a guided tour for groups can be arranged by appointment. The garden is semi-neglected, signalling that visits may be very infrequent. It is quite close to Villa Arson – the School of Fine Arts and National Contemporary Arts Centre on avenue Stéphen Liégeard.

The **Villa Arson – School of Fine Arts and National Contemporary Art Centre** is worth a visit from those particularly interested in cutting-edge visual art. A good way to get there is to take a tram ride from place Masséna (direction Las Planas), and alight at Le Ray stop. From there the college is but a short walk up the hill to the left.

The modern complex is built of concrete and clad with large river pebbles. It extends over a generous site, and the flat roof with flowers and spirals tops a series of confusing levels with rampart-like structures that are approached via a concrete labyrinth. It leads to high viewing points from which there are fine panoramic glimpses of the city and the Bay of Angels. Directly underneath is a Dominican church with a golden angel standing on the bell tower and an adjoining cemetery, and in the middle distance the pale slender spire of the modern church of Saint Joan of Arc can be discerned. The brutalist complex of teaching spaces, studios, library and administration contains some excellent 'white cubes' for exhibition purposes, designed by architect Michel Marot and built in 1972. A surround of pine trees lends a softening note to an otherwise unlovely brutalist environment.

Many works of modern art are dotted about the garden and buildings, some by well-known French artists. The list is impressive: Siah Armajani, Noël Dolla, Dan Graham, Ulrike Gruber, Bertrand Lavier, Francois Morellet, Maurizio Nannucci, Henri Olivier, Pascal Pinaud, Phillipe Ramette, Jean-Sebastian Tacher, Felice Varini, Michel Verjux. It takes a bit of detective work to find some of them, though there is a guide map posted on a noticeboard for the convenience of visitors.

The college cooperates with most of the art museums in the region, and appears to have useful contacts with the Ministry of Culture and the Pompidou Centre in Paris. On the two occasions when the author visited the campus, three art exhibitions were on view and they were of a good standard. All types of modern media are used, as one would expect, but traditional oil painting on canvas is still alive there and keeping the faith. In 2014 there were exhibitions by Jean-Yves Jouarnais, Grégory Castéra, Yaël Kreplak, Franck Leibovici, and Aurélien Froment, among others. Froment's very cool exhibition of photographed objects and wooden constructions, titled *Fröbel Fröbeled*, was co-produced with the Contemporary Art Gallery of Vancouver, Spike Island of Bristol, the FRAC Île-de-France-Le Plateau of Paris and the Heidelberger Kunstverein of Heidelberg. The atmosphere on the campus was friendly, open and welcoming.

Théâtre de la Photographie et de l'Image on boulevard Dubouchage has a series of smart exhibition spaces, and a film theatre that is a pleasure to visit. It was once a gentleman's club, possibly for artists only, since the theatre space is designated Salle de L'Artistique in memory of its former function. Apparently, many famous singers and dancers appeared there, some in the early stages of their careers before they became celebrities. These include Mata Hari and Isadora Duncan who met with a gruesome end soon afterwards. The space was transformed in 1999 into its present function. The exhibition rooms offer opportunities for all lens-based trends, from photojournalism to art photography, from traditional photography to digital images: portraits, landscapes, reporting, applied photography. It recently featured *Une Introspection*, a truly remarkable exhibition of the imaginative fashion drawings and subsequent coloured photograph images of Jean-Paul Goude, who is based in Paris. The son of Robert and Irene Goude of New York, he came to Paris where he fell in love with a young woman who did not return his affection. Thereafter, he drew a series of imagined images of her becoming pregnant, growing rounder monthly, and finally nestling her imaginary baby at her breast. This led on to a panorama of society figures against a white background that is very stark, but arresting.

The rooms displayed stunning sketches and photographs by Goude using top fashion models in a variety of imaginative poses and states of dress and undress. Grace Jones was the subject of some wonderful images. Other models who featured were Naomi Campbell, Linda Evangelista, Farida and the pop singer Björk. The artist has also made use of fashion designers John Galliano, Christian Lacroix, Thierry Mugler, Valentino, Jean Paul Gaultier and others to participate in his bizarre compositions. The theatre featured a film documenting the Paris celebrations in 1989 on the bicentenary of the French Revolution, and was a remarkable mélange of musicians, dancers and revellers, ranging from famed opera singer Jesse Norman to performing acrobats and Senegalese dancers in white dresses performing a riotous version of the ballet *Swan Lake*. A commentary in English and French alternated with excerpts from classical music by the great composers. Jean-Paul Goude was also exceptionally talented in major promotional videos made for top department stores and fashion products.

The venue also has a Documentations or Library Centre, a small bookshop selling postcards of old black-and-white photographs, and an interesting display of old cameras. Local Nice photographers of past fame, including Charles Negre, Jean Gilletta and Hercule Florence, are honoured with exhibition salons named after them. The artistic and cultural scene changes regularly in Nice, particularly during or after an economic recession. So it is of interest to notice that two new commercial art galleries recently opened for business in rue Maccarani beside the recommended gourmet restaurant Luc Salsedo. The first is **Darkroom Galerie**, which specialises in photographic exhibitions and the sale of limited editions. The second is **Galerie du Temple**, which exhibits modern art, artefacts and interior design furnishings. Both are situated opposite the Protestant Church, which was built in 1886 as the American Episcopal Church of the Holy Spirit.

Book market at place du Palais

La Grande Bibliothèque Louis Nucéra is a huge modern public library located in the extension to MAMAC on place Yves Klein. It occupies 10,000 square metres on a single level and has a half-dozen works of visual art on display in the foyer. Longtime Nice resident and artist Sacha Sosno (1937–2013) dominates with a white marble bust on a plinth of his famous image *La Tête Carrée*, 1994, a block head which was presumably the maquette for the massive thirty-metre-high square head of mesh and stone that dominates the **Jardin Maréchal Juin** at the rear. There is even a lithograph of the same head on view behind the administration desk, numbered from an edition of one hundred. The other local artist, also no longer alive, is Arman (Fernandez); installed on one of the walls is his fine encased *Assemblage of Open and Closed Books* sculpture. Nearby is a colourful abstract painting, artist not stated, which according to the receptionist could not be inspected up close. Near it is a more old-fashioned oil portrait of a man in his well-stocked library with his cat, signed illegibly and dated 2001, which may well be of bibliophile Louis Nucéra, after whom the library is named. The final work in the entrance area is a ten-foot carved wood sculpture, *Standing Man with his Head in a Book*, undocumented but presumably also by Sosno.

The library houses over 200,000 items and is freely open most days to registered members of the public. Unfortunately, this writer was not given permission to make a closer inspection of the works of art mentioned above, which were displayed behind a rope barrier. The Jardin Maréchal Juin behind the Nucéra Library is elaborately laid out with zigzag paths negotiating the stands of ancient olive trees and beds of colourful flowers. It also has flat concrete spaces on which young people skateboard during the day, before the entrance gate is closed. In addition, it contains a number of fine sculptures. The giant Sosno head in the corner at traverse Barla dominates, and is a key symbol of the city's modern architecture. *La Tête Carrée* (Square Head) houses the offices of the Louis Nucéra municipal library, but is not open to the public. It is constructed from steel mesh, concrete and other materials.

Opposite there is an admirable bronze sculpture, *Seated Giant with his Head in his Hands (L'Europe et la Mer)*, by prominent contemporary Italian trans-avant-garde artist Sandro Chia, who is well known internationally for his romantic figurative paintings and sculpture. He was born in Florence in 1946 but now lives mostly in New York. Nearby, there is a fine geometric abstract sculpture in rusting steel of the Antony Caro school of fabrication, though it does not carry an identifying attachment, it is by Jean-Claude Farhi (1940–2012). Further on there is a painted steel figure of a *Standing Man*, also unidentified, and after that a modestly-sized primitive figure fashioned from rocks and rusty iron by Max Cartier, dated 1990, and similar to his much larger piece in the same media which dominates the roundabout entrance to Nice airport. The garden is also worth a visit.

The next massive new building in the sequence of National Theatre, MAMAC and Nucéra Library is the **Acropolis**, built in 1984 on esplanade J. F. Kennedy. Functioning as one of the world's most impressive convention centres, it is surrounded by a number of commissioned sculptures, as might be expected in such a civilised country which fully appreciates the value of the arts. The Acropolis is approached from traverse Barla by a row of five circular fountains of varying sizes, all feeding in to an attractive water feature. On the corner is one of my favourite sculptures in Nice: *Nikaia*, a ten-foot draped female figure of welded steel, standing on a pedestal by local artist Volti. The front entrance to the Convention Centre on boulevard Risso is graced by three sculptures. The least interesting is *Nymphea*, 1995, by Michel Jarry, an unexceptional assemblage of bronze geometry. More impressive is the taller assemblage of sliced cellos titled *Music Power*, by Arman, cast in bronze and tapering towards an estimated twelve-foot apex, which is situated in the place of honour at the grand entrance. Further on, Sosno is again featured with his characteristic cast-bronze female figure, partially draped, and enclosed in two perpendicular blocks of white marble. It is of a similar height to the Arman. Its title *il faut en toute chose préférer l'intérieur à l'extérieur* (it is always better to prefer the inside to the outside).

There is a less attractive skeletal figure, made from iron bars by Pascal Morabito. Titled *Hommage à Biacelli*, 1985, it is inset under the cavernous structure. It is followed by a rather unattractive steel-like abstraction by Claude Gilli, titled *La couleur se déversant sur le pauvre monde*, also of 1985. The concept was three paint pots pouring their contents to the ground.

The final commissioned sculpture is sited on the far corner. *Les Trois Mondes* by Nice artist Noël Dolla, a member of the Supports-Surfaces movement, was fabricated in rusting steel plates in 1985 and features three large, roughly cut arrows, two of which point upwards while the centrepiece points to the ground. It is a well-realised piece of modern sculpture that has real presence. It looks across a square used for car parking, to the Acropolis Palais des Expositions,

visible behind the Novotel hotel. That large space is available for commercial purposes. A giant rusting steel sculpture, *Man with a Suitcase* by American artist Jonathan Borofsky (*b.* 1942), used to stand against the museum wall but is no longer there. Another cast of César's bronze sculpture *Le Pouce* (Thumb) is inside the Acropolis.

As one walks back to the Old Town from this newly built architectural conglomeration, one encounters the **Église Saint Jean-Baptiste-Le Voeu**, built by the Jesuits centuries ago. It is worth a quick visit to admire the grand altar, and the side chapels with impressive old paintings of religious subjects. The ceiling has some decoration but appears to have suffered damage, and is currently under repair. A special feature is the wonderful gilded baroque altar to Saint Mary Queen of Heaven.

After that, one should not neglect to pay a quick visit to **Basilica Notre-Dame** on ave Jean Médicin. It is the largest church in Nice and was built in 1864–68 after Nice became French. It was inspired by the Cathedral of Angers with its two square towers, and has really impressive stained-glass windows, including a glorious rose window with scenes of the Assumption. Artistically, the stained-glass is a must-see for art lovers. The windows are the work of three masters. The first is Champigneule, who made the nineteenth-century windows at floor level in 1896. The second is Maréchal, who made the stunning red and blue windows encircling the altar in the thirteenth-century manner. These two master craftsmen/artists collaborated in fabricating the windows from an atelier in Metz, though Champigneule was from Paris. The modern masters

were the Benôit brothers who made ten splendid abstract windows in 1956, five two-panel windows with rose overheads on each side of the Basilica, one set in blue and yellow and the other in red, green and yellow, reminiscent of the paintings of Mannessier. Apart from its religious services, the church is a regular venue for music recitals. The Basilica was refurbished in 2010.

Visitors interested in auctions might do well to inspect the premises of **Boisgirard & Associates** at 42, rue Gioffredo. Auctions of fine art are held here regularly, in association with Doyles of New York. For art lovers

on modest budgets, there is a coin and philatelic shop named **Vespa Philatelie** at 37, rue Gioffredo, where paintings and other works of art featuring on postage stamps may be purchased for modest prices, to form a collection in miniature.

Although I am primarily an enthusiast for avant-garde art, my favourite public sculpture in the whole of Nice – at least up to March 2015 – was the outstanding classical *Statue of Apollo*, carved from gleaming white Carrara marble and surrounded by five groups of energetic bronze figures in a grand circular *Fountain of the Sun*, occupying the place of honour in place Masséna. *Apollo* was apparently conceived and carved in 1934–37. The bronzes were modelled and cast later by the traditional French sculptor Alfred Auguste Janniot (1889–1969), and the ensemble was installed in 1956–57. Little is heard of Janniot nowadays but he was a big name in the first half of the twentieth century. He was educated at the École des Beaux-Arts in Paris and won the Prix de Rome in 1919. He came under the influence of the eminent French figurative sculptor Emile Antoine Bourdelle (1861–1929) and eventually became Professor of Monumental Art at the Beaux-Arts Academy in Paris from 1945 to 1959. He also did the carvings for the massive War Memorial near the port in Nice, and there is a sculpture by him, *c.*1930, on the façade of La Maison Française at Rockefeller Centre in New York City.

Apollo was the god of light and the sun in Greek mythology. He was also said to have many other attributes, being young, beardless, athletic, handsome, and devoted to music, poetry and fortune telling. He was the son of the great god Zeus and had a twin sister, Artemis. Janniot has portrayed him as a magnificently proportioned naked young man standing on top of a white marble pedestal in the middle

Apollo 1957 Alfred Auguste Janniot Carrara marble   61

of the vast circular fountain containing the five bronzes. He is seven metres tall, including the height of the pedestal, weighs six tonnes, as befits a great god, and reminds us of Michelangelo's even greater carving of *David* in Florence. It is said that Janniot based his composition on the *Fountain of Neptune* in Florence by Italian architect and sculptor Bartolomeo Ammannati (1511–92), who was much influenced by the art of Michelangelo. His right hand holds a draped garment and his left is extended as if in salutation to the five figures with animals beneath him in the water. These represent the planets or lesser gods of Mercury, Venus, Gaïa, Mars and Saturn.

The sculpture is perfectly placed, so that *Apollo* stands silhouetted against the azure sky and is framed by two ochre buildings in the square behind him, while he gazes imperiously across the place Masséna and down to the boulevard Masséna. He has a fine head of hair, presumably golden, crowned by a team of miniature prancing horses. This is where the history of this fine work of art becomes really interesting. The Greco-Roman myth had it that Apollo's daily task was to ferry the sun across the sky in his golden chariot drawn by four spirited horses. The artist took an understandable shortcut in delineating this, and symbolically placed the horses on the hero's head as a crown to remind everyone of the legend.

When the completed sculpture was inaugurated in 1956, to much fanfare, it did not meet with universal approval. Some citizens said that *Apollo's* genitals were too big, so the poor sculptor was obliged to chisel them down a centimetre or two to more modest proportions –

Venus, Mars, Saturn Alfred Auguste Janniot Three of five bronzes in the *Fountain of the Sun*

though he stopped short of emasculating him. Others were scandalised by the flagrant nudity of Vénus and Gaïa and their proximity to horned bulls and well-modelled rearing stallions. There was nothing the artist could do at this stage to alter the bronzes, despite the fact that Mars, Saturn and Mercury were equally well endowed, so they were left unchanged. *Apollo* was, sadly, removed in the 1970s to an obscure sports stadium location and not reinstalled until 2011, when he was finally restored to his proper place by crane, unveiled in the presence of the dynamic Christian Estrosi, Mayor of Nice and President of the Metropolitan Area. I remember witnessing the reinstallation. I had wondered why *Apollo* had been absent and where he had been stored, as the bronzes, though wonderful in themselves, seemed sadly incomplete without a towering figure. It is good to observe that the sculpture is nowadays probably the most photographed work of art in the city, and a regular backdrop for engaged and married couples. I am also very happy to relate that *Apollo's* genitals have suffered no further mutilation. On a sunny day the whole sculptural ensemble glitters as the fountains at *Apollo's* feet jet and splash vigorously over the green-patinated bronzes, which themselves were buried in the ground during the Second World War to avoid being melted down by the German army for their armaments programme.

The city of Nice constantly changes, and surprises us. In March 2015 I noticed that a new stone plinth had been sited in the **promenade du Paillon gardens** and wondered what new statue was destined for it. Picture my surprise when passing by a week later to spot a magnificent

bronze casting of Michelangelo's *David* standing on top of it. It is simply a glorious work of art that outshines every other sculpture, not only in Nice but throughout the entire French Riviera, including the one hundred sculptures to be seen in Monaco. Michelangelo has to be the greatest sculptor of all time, even taking account of Greek and Roman sculptors including the mighty Phidias. Like Janniot's *Apollo* sculpture a few hundred metres away, Michelangelo's colossal *David* stands almost six metres high, including the pedestal, and weighs 1.3 tonnes. Indeed, Janniot or a follower must have gone to Florence to see the original, because now the influence is close at hand for all to see. *David* dominates the centre of Nice, and it is an inspired choice. I wonder if his magnificent naked body with its rippling muscles and heroic masculinity will excite any residents to object as they did in 1956 to Janniot's *Apollo*? Most unlikely!

Michelangelo was commissioned to carve a sculpture to be placed on a buttress of Florence Cathedral, *c.* 1500. He began to carve this early masterpiece in 1501 and spent three years at his task, finishing the incredible work of art in 1504 at the age of twenty-nine. For his subject-matter he chose a biblical hero: the youthful shepherd boy who slew the giant Goliath with a slingshot. The result was a great Renaissance masterpiece that made his instant reputation and ensured he would never be without commissions from the highest in the land for the rest of his long life.

He ignored the initial brief and instead created a gigantic *David* (mimicking Goliath, who has his slingshot draped over his right fist). The enormous, energetic sculpture is 5.17 metres high, including its marble base, and features a standing male nude. The anatomical realisation is extraordinary, and unparalleled in the previous history of sculptural carving. The young engineer, architect, author, painter and sculptor knew full well that it would be too big and too heavy to hoist

David Michelangelo Bronze   Cast by art foundry Tesconi in Pietrasanta, Italy 1995

to the buttress on the cathedral, but he did not care. He was out to create a supreme work of art, releasing a miracle of realism from the huge block of stone, which he did magnificently. The original great work is now in the collection of the Accademia di Belle Arti de Firenze and is said to be the most admired of all the works there. A marble copy stands in a Florence square. This bronze casting in the promenade du Paillon was made in 1995 at art foundry Tesconi in Pietrasanta, Italy. It is the property of Nice art dealer Antonio Sapone, in whose presence it was unveiled on 6 March 2015 by the cultured mayor of Nice, Christian Estrosi. It is an extraordinary addition to the art of the city and becomes the yardstick against which all of the other sculptures on the Côte d'Azur will be judged. *David* is currently on loan to Nice for a three-year period. We can only hope it will remain permanently in Nice thereafter.

The promenade du Paillon where *David* is sited is a wonderful new broad path running through the heart of the city. Although only recently opened, it is proving to be hugely popular, particularly for its enormous new fountain of jets and periodic steam emissions. People, especially small children, flock to stand between the emissions and have their photographs taken. There are flower gardens and modern seating, and a handsome bronze sculpture of Jean Masséna by A. Carrier-Belleuse (1809–1909) on a large white marble plinth midway in the 12-hectare park which links the promenade des Anglais to MAMAC and the Théâtre de Verdure. An imaginative playground offers lots of features to occupy children.

I did state that I would only mention particular architectural favourites, as Nice has so many really splendid buildings that I could not do justice to them all. I must point out a few more at this stage. The **Palais des Ducs de Savoie**, dating from 1559 and facing onto the cours Saleya in the Old Town, is one of them. It is a grand baroque/neoclassical building that is still in public use and is designated a historic monument.

The **Chemins de Fer du Sud de la France** of 1892 is a simply glorious belle époque building in white and terracotta, embellished with busts and decorative stone ornaments. It stands out in a large open space with a fine stepped terrace to its front. This is still in use, selling tickets and acting as terminus for the Nice–Dignes-les-Bains monorail train service. The trip by the river Var through the mountains takes approximately four and a half hours to the historic Roman town of Dignes, and is unrivalled for scenery at all times of the year – whether in springtime when the mimosa is in blossom, or in autumn when, in the words of W.B. Yeats, *The trees are in their autumn beauty.*

General Charles de Gaulle, wearing his peaked cap and army uniform, commands the centre of **place Charles de Gaulle** near the monorail terminal. He stands, or rather strides, on a high plinth in the centre of the square, ruggedly cast in bronze by artist Jean Cardot and inaugurated by Christian Estrosi in 2011. The Riviera is simply full of tributes to this tall, dashing hero of France.

There is a small people's park to one side of the square, and in it we find another memorial to the French Resistance leader Jean Moulin, who is remembered elsewhere in Villefranche. On this occasion it is by means of an oval bronze plaque, carved in relief and set onto a

tilted slab of pink marble, supported and surrounded by six broken columns of marble. Moulin was a valourous hero who has elicited many memorials from his compatriots.

The **Église Sainte-Jeanne d'Arc**, a bit further on at 11, rue Grammont, is the most spectacular twentieth-century modern church building in Nice of which I am aware. The large, all-white building has a series of egg-shaped domes on the roof with narrow inset stained-glass windows, and beside it a soaring, thin white spire with bronze weathercock at its apex. At sixty-four metres high it is visible from most parts of the city, including the rooftop of the Villa Arson Art College. It is an avant-garde design from 1926–33 by Parisian architect Jacques Droz, who used reinforced slabs of concrete, upraised with strong supporting inner pillars, to realise his original vision starting from the shape of the egg – the source of all life. No wonder the parishioners have nicknamed it the 'church of the hard-boiled eggs'. From the outside the futuristic church has a decidedly oriental feel to it. From the inside the vast inner dome, with its multiple narrow stained-glass panels, is ultra-modern and calm. There are two good tapestries by Haitian artists and another from Mali, dated 1998, by Etienne Diarra de Kayes. Surprisingly, he chose the Russian artist Eugène Klementiev (1901–85) to paint the powerful but rather traditional frescoes, with a Russian-icon feel to the Stations of the Cross. The church is not always open but can be accessed at Mass times in the mornings and some evenings.

Notre-Dame-Auxiliatrice Saint-Jean-Bosco Church is a twentieth-century art deco church in the ancient Byzantine style. It was designed by Nice architects J. Febvre and M. Deporta and was inaugurated in 1933, the same year Droz's equally spectacular St Joan of Arc church was opened for worship. Though they compete for the accolade of the best modern church in Nice, they are very different from each other. While the St Joan of Arc church is all ovals and curves, Notre-Dame is all rectangles and squares. The latter is situated at 36, place Don Bosco. The massive interior fresco painting was entrusted to traditional Grasse artist Émile Doucet (1890-1978) and he did not finish the formidable task until some years later in 1946. The result was an enveloping blue canopy of a star-studded sky that is most uplifting and that complements the many elegant stained-glass windows celebrating the life of John Bosco, after whom the church is named.

One notices some fine buildings coming in along the **promenade des Anglais** from Nice airport. The first one that might catch your eye is the blue and beige upright modern **Hotel Nice Arénas** near the airport; it stands out because of the extraordinary colourful cubist sculpture *Dissémination*, 1990, by the exceptionally talented French artist Jean-Claude Farhi. The sculpture seems to hang from the top of the building, as if by magic, with nothing to support it but the genius of the artist. It is unlike any other sculpture on the Riviera and has attracted international attention. Farhi was such a good artist that he could move effortlessly from one form of expression to another, as he demonstrated by the great rusting steel piece on the roundabout at St-Paul de Vence.

Likewise, the Caryatid at **Villa Collin-Huovila** never fails to catch your
eye. An erotically modelled naked beige lady by Virieux seems to support
the wrought-iron balcony of this unique little art nouveau bijou residence
of 1907, sandwiched between more modern and clinical new buildings.

The sculptor Sosno's works are to be found in several locations around the
city, in addition to those already mentioned. His black-headed, relatively
small bronze figure titled *Les Sources de l'Aéropole* of 1992 at **Arénas** will
grab your attention, but his two great sensuous semi-nude casts of the
Virgin of the Elysée, set into the outer stone fabric of the modern luxury
hotel **Marriot Nice Hotel**, previously the **Elysée Palace**, on the
promenade des Anglais and backing onto the rue de France, will
simply stop you in your tracks. She is a giant dream-woman of the
Mediterranean beckoning to us all, yet quite remote as she gazes both
towards the hills and the sea. It is a most memorable, monumental,
modern double sculpture.

It's worth mentioning too that you can encounter works of art in
restaurants and smaller hotels as well as in museums and public places.
For example, the modest 3-star **Hôtel Windsor**, also known as
L'Hôtel des Artistes at 11, rue Dalpozzo in a quiet quarter of the
Musicians area, regularly holds exhibitions by local artists. Its guest
rooms have been decorated by different artists, and no two are the same.
A typical handwritten statement by Ben on an outside wall proclaims
the hotel's fascination with and receptivity to modern art. The **Safari
Restaurant** on the cours Saleya serves excellent food throughout the
day until midnight, and on special occasions stays open all night. It has
seating outside and inside, but the benefit of dining indoors is that you
can enjoy the many works of art on the walls, mostly drawings, just like
Langan's Brasserie in London which pursues a similar civilised policy.

The main **Jewish Synagogue** on rue Deloye was built in 1886 on the
site of a former theatre. Israeli-French Jewish artist Théo Tobiasse
(1927–2012), who painted somewhat in the manner of Marc Chagall,
was commissioned to design twelve stained-glass windows, which were
made in the glass studio of Alain Peirado in Nice. Like Chagall,
Tobiasse chose the Bible as his source for illustrations, and the theme
of his lyrical windows is the 'Song of the Prophets'.

Tobiasse showed his art extensively in France and the USA. And he decorated the small Saint-Sauveur chapel in Le Cannet around the motto: *Life is a Celebration.* He was born in Jaffa and as a child was brought to Paris from Israel, where he made his earliest drawings before embarking on a successful career as a painter and printmaker.

The exciting thing about Nice is that it is constantly upgrading its buildings and facilities. It also regularly expands its artistic heritage, mainly thanks to the generosity of private owners but also to the foresightedness and affection for their city of the municipal authorities. Recently, the Museum of Modern and Contemporary Art (MAMAC) got an important donation of over sixty modern works of art by a private collector, Mr Berggren, and publicly exhibited them. One particularly noteworthy donation, of 853 works by the School of Nice artists, was made by art gallery owner and photographer Jean Ferrero (*b.* 1931). His father was Italian, his mother French, and he grew up with and photographed many of the local artists he collected. His donation is hugely generous. A selection of these works was exhibited in 2014 at the **Ancien Forum de l'Urbanisme** beside the cours Saleya in central Nice. The collection will be rotated over time, as it is too extensive to be shown in full at that limited space, which looks like a former fire station. There is a possibility the collection will move to a more suitable permanent venue in due course. I feel sympathy for the journalist who exclaimed some years ago, 'Not another art gallery on the Riviera', but I am glad for all true lovers of the visual arts that the trend continues.

The very beautiful old **Chapelle de la Très-Sainte Trinité et du Saint-Suaire** (Holy Trinity and Holy Shroud Chapel) at the very end of the cours Saleya could easily be missed or ignored, as it is rarely open. But it is worth making the effort to visit it for the Latin Mass at 10 am on Sunday, if only to view the treasures it contains. It belongs to the Red Penitents confraternity, and the lay people who assist the priests at Mass all wear dark red soutanes. It was built in the late baroque style and is said to have been partly restored by the Italian architect Giovanni Battista Borra in 1763. The triangle on the façade represents the Holy Trinity. The exterior may be fairly plain, but the interior is glorious. It contains a number of fine antique paintings and some spectacular stucco work, together with impressive statues and some unusual features. The major painting on the left-hand side of the nave portrays *Christ in the Tomb*, with Mary and the Disciples grieving over his death and holding the Holy Shroud of Turin. It dates from 1660 and is said to have been painted by a local artist named Jean-Gaspard Baudoin, whom I have not encountered elsewhere. On the opposite wall is an even better painting of Christ with his hands tied, wearing a red garment. It is smaller but was painted by a very accomplished artist – perhaps one of the Brea brothers? The altar is very ornate, with tall brass candlesticks adorning its marble top. Above it is another fine painting of the *Crucified Christ with God the Father*. The Father looks down from heaven, clothed in blue and red, which contrasts dramatically with the pale flesh of His Son on the cross. A massive carved Christ on the Cross hangs suspended in front of the altar, surrounded by polychromed decorations. The Stations of the Cross are quiet polychromed reliefs. Inside the door, in an alcove to the right, is a statue of St Hospice about to be slain by a Roman soldier with upraised sword, while polychromed sympathisers look on. On the other side is a competent medium-sized painting that appears to be *Christ Preaching in the Temple*. The church was crowded for Sunday Mass during my visit. It was opened for public visits for two weeks in June 2014, probably to elicit contributions towards further refurbishment. It is a gem of a church, lovingly looked after by its faithful parishioners.

In 2015 Nice introduced a new system of admission fees for entry to municipal museums in the city. A €20 ticket will give you entrance to them all, valid for one week. An individual ticket now costs €10. A ticket for MAMAC entitles you also to visit six related museums within a forty-eight hour period. A €10 ticket for the Matisse Museum entitles you likewise to visit six other municipal museums if you produce the ticket at entrance within the forty-eight hour validity period. Usage is marked off on the ticket. Non-municipal museums such as the Chagall and the Maeght Foundation are outside of the system and control their own substantial admission charges. The only free entry to the municipal museums is on the first Monday of every month.

This system makes it expensive to follow the art trail. Nice has thirteen art museums, but you would be busy for a week if you decided to visit them all in one week to get the best value for your €20 admissions ticket.

Nice is a unique city for art lovers to visit. It has so many museums, so many ancient and modern churches with important works of art, so many commercial art galleries, so many fine buildings and public sculptures, that you could spend an entire holiday here exploring art, and not find time to visit the many superb art museums further up and down the coast. That would be a mistake. Perhaps the solution is to pick and choose and make frequent visits, as this writer has done over the years.

Bear in mind that many museums are dynamic institutions that either vary their permanent collections regularly or show contemporary art also from time to time. You can never be sure what you will encounter next, but you can be certain that it will be vibrant and interesting. For example, you might enter a small antiques shop on rue Alberti and be tempted to purchase an African mask, or even be offered a drawing by Picasso. You might even go for an aperitif in a bar on the rue d'Angleterre and encounter writers and artists.

Wherever you go in Nice, you will generally be met with the utmost courtesy, particularly if you make a reasonable attempt at speaking the language, either French or Nikaia, the local dialect which is still very much alive and in use. Nice proudly displays its roots, which stretch back to Greek and Roman settlements before becoming an Italian province and ultimately part of France from the mid-nineteenth century. Today it welcomes tourists from all over the world, and it has such a lot to offer them.

> *When I realised that every morning I would see this light, I couldn't believe my luck.*
>
> *Henri Matisse*

The sprawling seaside city of Cagnes-sur-Mer has two major art attractions, the **Musée Renoir** and the **Château Grimaldi**. Cagnes-sur-Mer is a short bus or train journey from Nice. The number 400 bus starts outside the Méridien Hotel in Nice and gets you to the centre of Cagnes in about half an hour. After that you have to walk for ten minutes, part of it uphill, to reach the former residence of the great artist Pierre-Auguste Renoir (1841–1919) at La Domaine des Collines. It is well signposted. It is a smart new museum with facilities for car parking and a shop that sells books, prints and postcards, attractively displayed. The orangerie and ancient olive grove on the sloping terraces are extremely well maintained, and the public is encouraged to wander about them. In 1907, Renoir purchased *Les Collettes* and built a house in stone and mortar for the greater comfort of his wife, Aline. She died eight years later and he outlived her by a mere four years.

There is an admission charge of €6 per adult. The major difference between this new museum and the rambling house that I visited some years ago is that it now contains a satisfactory number of paintings by the master, instead of the few scraps that were left there at the end of his life. Most of the paintings have been lent by the Musée d'Orsay in Paris. In addition, a substantial amount of family material has been purchased by the town of Cagnes-sur-Mer at a recent heritage auction in New York, and this adds greatly to the enjoyment of the visit. The ground floor of the museum is devoted to sculpture and some family photographs. It was here that the great romantic painter first experimented with sculpture at the insistence of his friend Auguste Maillol, who sculpted Renoir's portrait. Because Renoir's hands were arthritic at this late stage in his career, it was impossible for him to carve or model completely by himself. So he did it by proxy, using a long stick and giving detailed instructions to a skilled young Spanish sculptor, Richard Guino, whom Maillol had trained in Paris. The results are very impressive. A larger-than-life plaster of *La Grande Lavreuse* (Big Washerwoman) is credited to Renoir and Guino, inspired by a small oil painting by Renoir, titled *Lavreuse*, that has been lent by the Beaux-Arts Museum of Lyon. Three bronze busts of considerable presence are on view from the same partnership. The busts are of the painter's wife, Aline, in 1916, a year after she had died.

Renoir collaborated with another sculptor, named Louis Morel, to produce terracotta relief portraits in 1918, just a year before his own death. It is said that Renoir was able to complete only two small bronze sculptures unaided; both are portraits of his young son Claude, known as Coco, in 1907 and 1908. One of these, a charming relief, is featured on the back of the admission ticket.

Upstairs now has a number of paintings by Renoir on view, thanks to the Musée d'Orsay in Paris. The most impressive is the large *Les Grandes Baigneuses* of 1903–05 featuring four well-rounded pretty females, painted with all the richness of colouring and modelling of form of which the master was capable in his prime. There is also a beautiful little painting from 1915 of the clock tower in Nice, unsigned; it captures the architecture and atmosphere of the Old Town most successfully.

The Grand Atelier upstairs displays Renoir's wheelchair beside his easel, paints and brushes, as if he might re-enter the room at any moment and begin to paint again. Indeed, a painting on the wall by his friend Albert André in 1916 depicts just that. Renoir continued painting up to the year he died, 1919. By this stage brushes had to be strapped to his arthritic hands.

In another room is a charming small painting *Bal au Moulin de La Galette d'après Renoir* by Raoul Dufy (1877–1953) as well as some more portraits of Renoir by his friends. Downstairs hangs the impressive Cariatides painting of two standing female nudes, again lent by Musée d'Orsay. Beside it is a ravishing small, unfinished sketch titled *Nu Assis*.

Relief portraits 1918 Pierre-Auguste Renoir Terracotta

Les Grandes Baigneuses
1887
Pierre-Auguste Renoir
Oil on canvas

The garden contains a bronze cast of a voluptuous Venus on a plinth, and near it a cast of the full-length, well-rounded standing nude known as *Venus Victrix*. The garden still has wonderful views of the sea in the distance, where yachts can sometimes be glimpsed.

To the right there is still a fine view of the Château Grimaldi, despite all the new building that has taken place in the valley below since the artist's death. A visit to the Renoir Museum is now a nostalgic and worthwhile experience.

In the centre of Cagnes-sur-Mer, if you are observant and curious, you will discover a most attractive carved stone, *Reclining Female Nude*, under a spreading evergreen tree. Appropriately enough, it is a homage to Renoir by the artist Bouraine from Biot.

Haut-de-Cagnes, the old town on the steep hilltop where the **Château-Musée Grimaldi** is situated, is best reached by a free Navette service which runs up and down the hill every ten minutes or so, if you are lucky. Be aware that the museum closes for a two-hour lunch break at noon, though lunch on the high terrace at Le Jimmy's can be enjoyable in the sun during the interval. The views from the

Renoir's wheelchair beside his easel, paints and brushes

Roman relief
sculpture
Château Grimaldi

high terrace are once again spectacular.
The château was built by the powerful
nobleman, Rainier Grimaldi, in the
fourteenth century and only became a
museum in 1946. One of its interesting
features is a 200-year-old pepper tree
still growing in an inner courtyard.
The château has an olive oil museum,
a Suzy Solidor museum, a series of
rooms of some nondescript landscapes
and donations by visiting and local
artists, and a space on the top floor for
periodic exhibitions of important
contemporary art.

The Suzy Solidor Donation consists of forty portraits of the
androgynous blonde model, singer and antiques dealer made by
different artists the sitter encountered over the years. Solidor was
born Suzanne Rocher in St Malo in the north of France in 1900, and
changed her name upon moving to Paris. After a colourful career as a
cabaret artist mixing in the bohemian milieu, she retired to Haut-de-
Cagnes in 1960 where she sold jewellery and antiques. She must have
had a remarkable personality to be able to persuade so many artists,
famous and not so famous, to paint her – she accumulated 224 portraits
of herself during her lifetime. The mind boggles as to how she was able
to reward the artists for their work. The quality of the portraits varies.
Of particular note are Jean Cocteau's lively drawing of her in 1937,
Tamara de Lempicka's saucy half-length portrait of her with bare
breast, Tsuguharu Foujita's splendid full-length portrait of Suzy
kneeling beside a large dog, and Marie Laurencin's characteristic
half-length portrait in soft, pastel colours. Solidor posed nude for
several portraits, and was even sculpted in bronze by a few artists.

The château's permanent collection, though very mixed, has some
good works on view, donated by local residents. These include paintings
by the American Paul Jenkins (1923–2012), the French Sacha Sosno
(1937–2013), the Italian Ben, the French Jean Miotte, the Japanese

Tsuguharu Foujita (1886–1968) and the Russian Moïse Kisling (1891–1955). Kisling's tiny oil painting of a pink rose in a black vase against a green background is a small unexpected masterpiece.

The top floor has attractive exhibition rooms and features occasional retrospectives. The main reason the Grimaldi Museum is well known is because for many years it held an International Festival of Painting, which was sponsored by UNESCO. Every country in the world was invited to send works by two young artists to the exhibition, paid for by each participating country. Prizes were awarded annually, judged by a committee of up to eight art critics and curators, chosen through an opaque system of rotation, favouring the French.

Young Irish artists participated in this exhibition for many years and met with some success. Camille Souter HRHA (*b.* 1929) once won the top prize for her moody Irish landscapes. Richard Gorman RHA (*b.* 1946) won the Palette d'Or prize as a young man, when this writer was a member of the jury, nominated by the Irish Department of Foreign Affairs. Nowadays such matters are handled for Ireland by Culture Ireland, and it concentrates on the Venice Biennales, which are considered more important outlets for aspiring young artists than the more conservative Cagnes-sur-Mer exhibitions. Nevertheless, Cagnes benefited greatly over the years from the annual influx of tourists and artists. The festival has recently been superseded by a new programme of exhibitions.

Château Grimaldi is, of course, a historic monument which deserves to be preserved and put to good use. Its attached **Église St-Pierre** dates from the thirteenth century and is open to the public after lunch. It has some colourful stained-glass windows and older religious paintings which cannot be viewed closely because of the gloom in the old building and the lack of lights. The main exhibition in the church in 2014 was a display in glass cases of thirty-seven old folk dolls of the region, dressed in bright clothes of the period 1820–50.

The 360-degree view from the tower on top of the château is a magnificent vista that should not be missed. You can see almost as far

as the Italian border on one side and down to Cannes and beyond to
Saint-Tropez on the other. Behind are the encircling mountains with
their colourful hilltop villages dotted about them. Its only rival for
such a fine, extensive view might be the hilltop botanical garden
over Èze Village.

Art lovers will find much to interest them at **Polygone**, where they
will encounter arresting works of modern art skillfully placed
throughout the complex. Distinguished French art director Jérome
Sans has responsibility for choosing the artists and the art, and he
has done extremely well at the outset, including major paintings,
sculptures and installations by eleven celebrated international artists.
These include César, Daniel Buren, Antony Gormley, Jean-Michel
Othoniel, Pascale Marthine Tayou and Sacha Sosno, the
reporter-turned-sculptor and Riviera resident whose family name
was Alexandre Joseph Sosnowsky.

Sosno's massive new work, *Le Guetteur* (The Watcher), is the standout
sculpture. It is an amazing dominant block-clad sliced cube of a
building with a giant pale partial male classical head in the middle and
supporting the upper level. The concept could just have been that of a
massive cubist sponge cake made from black limestone with a seeming
pale glass face as the filling between the two layers, though of course
the face is constructed or cast from much more durable material than
glass. Not only does it function as a remarkable and beautiful new
work of art, but it also houses the administrative staff of the centre
on its upper level and a Maotsumy restaurant on its lower level.
Apparently, there are wonderful views of land and sea from the flat
rooftops of the sculpture building. Sosno was obsessed with square head
shapes, and his giant aluminium landmark *Tête Carrée* in Nice houses
the administrative staff of the modern Nucéra Municipal Library.

A forerunner of this new work can be seen near La Porte de L'Arénas
beside the airport in Nice, where there are many public sculptures.
The art commissioner Jérome Sans is well qualified for his new job,
having organised art exhibitions in Paris, Taipei, Milan and Lyon as
well as directing the well-known Ullens Centre for Contemporary Art

(UCCA) in Beijing from 2008 to 2012. He promises to change the exhibitions at Polygone every six months, which is something to look forward to, though I will miss the large transparent cubic outdoor sculpture, constructed ingeniously from simple wire coathangers. Sosno's outstanding work, of course, is a permanent one and will remain the signature sculpture of Polygone.

The centre has parking spaces for up to 3,000 vehicles and is also well served by public transport. The number 57 bus travels frequently between the centre and the Gare Centrale of Cagnes-sur-Mer.

Le Guetteur 2015 Sacha Sosno (sculptor) and Yves Bayard (architect) Aluminium, black limestone and glass

I had an early aversion to the paintings of Fernand Léger (1881–1955), as I did to the paintings of English artist William Roberts, finding their figurative art too 'tubular' and mechanistic for my taste.

It is a view shared by some of my friends, who decided against visiting the Léger Museum at Biot, near Antibes, when we were exploring the area some years ago. Instead, we drove up the hill to Biot village and visited the glass-blowing factories and exhibitions before eating a gourmet meal washed down with excellent wine of the region.

We all missed a wonderful art opportunity.

I decided soon afterwards to visit the Léger Museum alone. I took the number 200 bus for Cannes at the Méridien Hotel in Nice, alighting at the Gare de Biot stop just short of Antibes forty-five minutes later. Along the way I marvelled at the complex of four huge curved apartment blocks that look from a distance like a gathering of giant cruise liners corralled together on the beach at Loubet Marina. These modern tiered buildings are complete with rooftop gardens. They can usually be seen from incoming flights during the day because they are such a prominent feature of the Riviera landscape, and on incoming night flights they can appear as a gossamer necklace of bright, winking lights. It took me twenty minutes to walk to the Léger Museum from the bus stop, with a brief digression to view a bric-a-brac market and to look in the window of **Verrerie du Val de Pôme**. I set aside the nearby Musée du Bonsaï and Arboretum for another day. When I turned the corner and the Léger Museum came into sight I was entranced by the beauty and bright forms and colours of the vast ceramic-mosaic frieze that adorns the entire museum façade. This was the first of several visits I have since made to what is one of the handsomest modern buildings on the French Riviera, and contrary to my initial impression it is full of treasures also. I have happily been forced to revise my opinion of the art of Fernand Léger. He is one of the modern greats.

The **Musée National Fernand Léger** on chemin du Val de Pôme is a five-minute walk uphill after the bridge over the motorway, on the

Musée National
Fernand Léger

main road leading up to Biot village. The museum is open daily
except on public holidays. There is a modest admission charge of
about €4.50 and it is very good value for money. Visitors from Antibes
can catch the number 14 Envibus from the town centre and be at the
roundabout in fifteen minutes. Visitors from anywhere else on the
Riviera can also access it by train, bus, or car. The museum has ample
car parking facilities at the road side of the building, facing three
massive, bright mosaic panels by Léger. The centre one is titled
Les Oiseaux sur Fond Jaune and it is flanked on either side by two
equally impressive abstract compositions. Entrance to the museum
has been rerouted, from the original gated direct route to an attractive
winding footpath from the car park. This ensures that visitors get
changing views of the different mosaic friezes and garden sculptures
before they reach the main entrance.

The front frieze was designed by Léger for the Olympic stadium in
Hanover before he died suddenly in 1955, a mere fifteen days after
purchasing this substantial site near Biot on which he proposed to
build an atelier. These mosaics were his main concern in his final year,
and many of them now grace the surrounding garden. Léger loved to
spend time on this site surrounded by shady pine trees and alive with

birdsong and colourful butterflies in spring and summer. He was extremely well served by his second wife, Nadia, and his devoted studio assistant, Georges Bauquier, who between them donated 285 works by the deceased artist to the museum they had built in 1960: forty-eight paintings, sixty-eight gouaches, a few dozen drawings and lithographs, more than thirty ceramic sculptures, a number of large bronzes, and some truly great modern tapestries. André Malraux, then French Minister of Culture, came down to Biot to officially accept the generous donation to the State. Nadia chose the Russian architect André Svetchine from Nice, who designed the modern, decorated geometric building to display some of the artist's greatest works. It was first built forty-five metres long and thirteen metres wide and at once became a perfect vehicle in which to display Léger's art: the various forms were in perfect harmony with the architecture. It was enlarged in 1989 to provide more space for additional donations, and work seems to be ongoing since then to upgrade the gardens and maintain the sculptures and mosaics that can suffer slight damage during winter storms.

Léger's large upright polychrome sculpture *Jardin d'Enfance* is judiciously sited like a sentinel in the shade of the pine trees and facing the façade of the museum. Beside it on a green lawn is *La Buvette du Musée*, where tasty snacks can be purchased and consumed indoors or alfresco in the sun.

Although the museum is not very large, it manages to put on varied exhibitions of the artist's work. On one of my visits, the main exhibition space on the ground floor showed one of his larger masterpieces, the painting *Les Constructeurs* of 1950, accompanied by many drawings and gouache preparatory studies of building workers clambering about the steelwork of a skyscraper under construction. It was probably inspired by his visits to America and his love of the dignity of ordinary people. On a subsequent visit, the space was devoted to tapestries woven over the years at Aubusson ateliers by skilled artisans working from the artist's gouache studies. These are simply wonderful works of collaborative art. Amazingly, most of them were woven after the artist's death, no doubt overseen by his devoted assistant, Georges Bauquier, and of course by his loving widow, Nadia.

Fernand Léger (1881–1955) was born in Normandy and began painting in a post-impressionist figurative manner before he came under the influence of the great Paul Cézanne and then later of the originators of cubism, Pablo Picasso and Georges Braque. He subsequently became friendly with Marcel Duchamp and his two Villon artist brothers, but soon felt he had to break away from all of their influences to develop his own unique style. For a time he consorted in Paris with second-wave cubists such as Gleizes, Delaunay-Terk, Picabia and Kupka and tried to be an abstract, geometric painter; he succeeded in 1926 when he painted *Composition Murale*, a large, upright, geometric composition with precise rectangles of dark red and green and vertical bands of sober colour on a grey ground, somewhat reminiscent of the Russian suprematist Kasimir Malevich (1879–1935) and anticipating the rigid modernist sculptures of Donald Judd some fifty years later.

From 1930 onwards he was again painting in a decidedly figurative vein, glorying in the sensuous naked female form and creating unique combinations of humans in natural surroundings that could appear somewhat clumsy but in fact were powerful juxtapositions of simplified forms and contrasting strong colours.

Les Acrobats, 1942–46, is a very successful composition of entangled athletes powerfully outlined in black, and painted entirely in a nuanced shade of Mediterranean blue. It reminds me that Léger himself was a hulking great bulk of a man, with a bodily frame built like a professional wrestler. Typical of the artist's late work, where he glorifies the common people about their pursuits, is *Les Loisirs sur Fond Rouge*

of 1949, the acclaimed large painting of a family on a day out in the countryside with their bicycles, taking a brief rest beside an agave plant against a background of a red sky with a single small cloud. Likewise impressive is *La Partie de Campagne*, dated 1953, a monumental study of people about to picnic in the countryside. Though it appeared on one visit it was not on view a year later, presumably having been taken back into the store. No one else could have painted like that except Léger. Indeed, no one else ever made such bright, simplified relief sculptures in a variety of media like Léger did. You cannot leave the Léger Museum without experiencing the two wonderful large tapestries that hang there. These are a big surprise and delight. Outstanding is the very large *Les Baigneuses (The Bathers)*, woven at Ateliers Gisèle Glaudin-Brivet in Aubusson in 1962 for the extended front entrance of the museum. It overhangs and dominates the reception counter and shop. Flanking it on one side, over the stairs, is another fine tapestry, *Ciel de France*, also woven in 1962 in Aubusson but this time by Atelier Pinton Frères. *Bathers* is flanked on the other side by a matching large stained-glass window of red and black abstract design, fabricated in Lausanne after the master's design. The great *Bathers* tapestry features four massive naked females lying and kneeling in a tight intertwined composition of great power and grandeur. The artist's widow, Nadia, commissioned it in 1980 to be made from an enlarged gouache drawing by Léger, dated

1953. This unique, low-toned composition of four bathing females, outlined in strong black lines with subtle grey shading on a plain beige background is a triumph of art. The tragedy is that the creator did not live long enough to see his little masterpiece transposed and transformed. The museum possesses a smaller weaving of the *Bathers* from the same atelier, and it is equally attractive and compelling.

If you decide to go to the top of the hill and visit the colourful old village of Biot, you will be rewarded with other works of interest. The old church with the Pénitents Noirs Tower contains two admirable antique paintings: *Retable du Rosaire* by Nice master Ludovico Brea, painted in red and gold, and *Christ aux Plaies* by Jean Giovanni Canavesio, *c.* 1500.

There is also a small museum in the walled town on rue Saint-Sebastian celebrating the ceramics industry which has flourished here for centuries, due to the suitable clay available locally. It is known as **Le Musée d'Histoire et de Céramique Biotoises** and it contains specimens of ceramic art and some hundreds of photographs donated by local citizens over the years. The village also has craft shops selling leather goods and glassware. Biot is famous for its bubble glassworks, and visitors can observe the glassworkers blowing the glass in the factory **La Verrerie de Biot** before moving on to the sales area, where attractive wares are available. Across the road is the **Écomusée de Verre**, which has an impressive display of blown-glass sculptures by international artists; most items are available for purchase.

The Biot experience can be capped by a pleasant lunch or dinner in the centre of the picturesque village, with its excellent restaurants and many souvenirs of an ancient past. If you are using public transport, the local bus will drop you back down to Antibes afterwards by a fascinating circuitous route in about fifteen minutes.

The craving for colour is a natural necessity just as for fire and water.   *Fernand Léger*

Antibes

Antibes is one of the most colourful and enjoyable cities to visit on the
French Riviera. It has an ancient history, starting as a Greek trading outpost
named Antipolis, literally the 'city opposite' (opposite Nice further up the
coast). In the 1920s it was the playground for holidaying rich Americans,
including Zelda and Scott Fitzgerald and Sara and Gerald Murphy, as well
as a favourite stamping ground for many other artists, now famous, including
Pablo Picasso, Hans Hartung and his wife Anna-Eva Bergman, and Nicolas
de Staël. These are represented today by excellent works in the **Picasso
Museum**, which is the capital venue on your art agenda on a first visit to
Antibes. Sadly, it does not have a painting by the American socialite Gerald
Murphy, who was richly talented as well as rich in reality; only six large
quasi-cubist figurative canvases by this eccentric artist of Irish extraction
have survived, and they are all in America.

Pablo Picasso (1881–1973) was born in Málaga, Spain, though he spent
most of his adult life in France. He showed extraordinary artistic talent from
an early age and was accomplished in a variety of media - painting, sculpture,
ceramics, printmaking, stage design and writing poetry and plays. From the
late 1940s he lived in the south of France. In 1961 he moved to Mougins
where he continued his prolific work until his death at the age of ninety-two.

The Picasso Museum is situated on the ramparts facing out to the sparkling
blue Mediterranean Sea and just a series of steps up from cours Masséna, the
main street of the ancient city. The modest admission charge, with half price
for senior citizens, is well worth it: this is one of the best museums
on the French Riviera. The museum has had an interesting history. The
Grimaldis built the castle in 1385 on the site of the Greek settlement, and
that family ruled Antibes until 1608. Centuries later the municipality bought
the castle in a ruined state and dubbed it the **Grimaldi Museum**. In 1928 it
was classified as a historic monument. In 1946 the curator Romuald Dor
de la Souchère proposed to Pablo Picasso that he should consider using the
second floor as a studio. The artist gladly accepted, as he was living in the

*Antibes is only an hour's journey by the number 200 bus from Nice, and much
shorter by train. It is also very close to Juan-les-Pins and quite close to Cannes.*

vicinity with his artist lover Françoise Gilot and had investigated the ruined castle as a possible venue for painting large works. It resulted in Picasso spending two months there painting and drawing in his inimitable frenzied fashion. The citizens recognised a golden opportunity and thereupon dedicated the castle to the artist in 1947, after which Picasso donated twenty-three paintings and forty-four drawings.

Among these are two major masterpieces, both from 1946, which are still on view there today: the idyllic oil painting *La Joie de Vivre* and *Ulysses and the Sirens*, painted and drawn on three panels of fibro-cement building materials. Another supreme example of Picasso's extreme virtuosity is the much cooler *Les Clefs d'Antibes* of 1946, painted directly onto the damp inner wall of the castle. A rectangle and two circles were drawn in charcoal and brushed with industrial paint onto an end wall in what might have ended as an abstract geometric composition, except that figurative artist Picasso could not restrain himself from including within the forms minimal images of a human face (perhaps his own). It was also a time of scarcity after the Second World War, so Picasso, lacking new canvases, bought and found old paintings of no great artistic value in local shops and painted over them with enamel paint.

The building only officially became the Picasso Museum in 1966, after the artist had donated further tranches of beautiful works in 1948 and 1954. The room that now contains *Ulysses and the Sirens* also displays fifty-two magnificent examples of Picasso's wonderful decorated ceramic plates. One wall has sixteen plates on the theme of birds, while a second wall has three rows of nine on the themes of bull-fighting, birds, fruits, eggs, and of course faces. The artist's inventive mastery of this new medium at the Madoura Pottery in nearby Vallauris is breathtaking. There is, of course, a commercial **Galerie Céramique du Château** just outside the museum selling limited editions of Picasso ceramics at considerable prices for those with the interest – and deep pockets!

The museum has rooms displaying Picasso's effortlessly amazing drawings. The final work which always catches my eye is the oil and graphite painting *Buste d'homme au chapeau* of 1972, donated by the artist's wife, Jacqueline, in 1990. It is surely a self-portrait of the nonagenarian, two years before his death, painted as something of an imagined musketeer after an event-filled

life. It is as affecting as the two great plaster sculptures of 1932, standing on plinths in the *Ulysses* room. These are two vigorously modelled twisted profiles of a woman with a prominent nose that display absolute mastery of three-dimensional forms.

The Picasso Museum also displays some master paintings by the Russian artist Nicolas de Staël (1914–55), who lived around the corner and sadly died by suicide at an early age. In 2014 the museum put on a very large exhibition of de Staël's paintings and drawings, many of them borrowed from private collections, to mark the centenary of the artist's birth. It revealed a wonderful colourist who blurred the distinction between figure and abstraction in his short working life, and who attracted controversy before and after his death. He was born in St Petersburg, the son of an aristocratic Russian general, just three years before the Bolshevik Revolution. After this the family fled Russia, first to Poland and then to spend his childhood in Belgium, before visiting North Africa and eventually settling in Paris in 1938. During the Second World War he joined the French Foreign Legion and saw service in Tunisia.

Photographs of the artist in his Parisian studio by Denise Colomb reveal a gauntly handsome, melancholy man who despaired at the Nazi occupation of his adopted city, and was moved to paint initially in dark earth colours in the 1940s. The paintings in the Picasso Museum show him turning to vibrant colour in the 1950s when he experienced the bright light of the Riviera and enjoyed the friendship of his mentor, the great Georges Braque. They also show that he preferred the palette knife to the brush. He was apparently a follower of rugby football, as demonstrated by the wonderful large oil painting *Parc des Princes* of 1952, together with some smaller studies. Here, he blends human forms into patches of colour that integrate into a dynamic abstract composition of forms and shapes. Outstanding also, with colours that sing, was a modestly sized canvas of 1954 from a private collection, after he had moved to the south of France and experienced the tropical colours of Antibes. The largest painting by the artist in the permanent collection of the museum is *Le Concert* dated March 1955, a gigantic, colourful canvas occupying an entire wall. A black piano to the left is balanced by a huge cello image in ochre to the right, with the orchestra members hinted at in the middle against a deep red background. It is a haunting, wonderful painting, completed a short time before his death. He left a widow and children behind to mourn him. In his short career he also made many drawings of the female form and of musical occasions and had a rare facility with ink and brush, reminiscent of Matisse at his most fluent.

The final pair of important modern painters on permanent display at the Picasso Museum are Hans Hartung (1904–89) and Anna-Eva Bergman (1909–87). In 2001 the Fondation Hartung-Bergman donated thirty-six works by Hartung and eight paintings by Bergman

The studio of Hans Hartung

to the Picasso Museum for permanent display on its ground floor. Hartung's brilliant grainy vertical black brushstrokes over yellows and blue, *T1976–R39*, of 1976 stands out in the display and echoes the painting of French master Pierre Soulages (*b.* 1919). Bergman's no. 50 *Pyramide d'Argent sur fond d'Argent Gris* of 1962 and *Grand Nunatak* painting of 1974, using silver and gold leaf with acrylic, are beautiful paintings that echo the work of Irish artist Patrick Scott (1921–2014), who used similar materials to attain equally beautiful results.

We cannot leave the Picasso Museum without viewing the many fine sculptures at the back of the building and at (or on) the ramparts. Germaine Richier (1902–59) is represented by four typical emaciated standing figures in bronze and two abstracts carved from Flanders stone. Joan Miró (1893–1983) is represented by a number of painted metal sculptures, some of which have been lent by the Maeght Foundation at St-Paul de Vence. Of particular appeal is Miró's *Femme et Oiseau*, a tall bronze sculpture of 1982 at the entrance to the museum. In the courtyard is an impressive tower of bronze cellos by Arman, titled *À Ma Jolie* and dedicated in homage to Picasso. There is the admirable, massive simplicity of Bernard Pagès's *La Colonne d'Antibes*, 1983–84, made from bricks, stone, marble and cement. Finally, don't miss the unusual assemblage of stones and marble carvings of two huge eyes, with a giant bronze arrow embedded in the earth, appropriately titled *Jupiter et Encelade*, 1982–83, by Anne and Patrick Poirier. It is not your conventional type of sculpture. After such a feast of modern art, I recommend a break for lunch before viewing other museums. Near the harbour is Restaurant Vaubon which is run by a husband and wife team who cook great food.

Fondation Hartung-Bergman is located at 173 chemin du Valbosquet, just outside Antibes. I recommend you visit as the beautiful art, the Minorcan-inspired architecture and its setting in the silent sloping ancient olive grove, is a deeply enriching experience.

It is open only on Fridays at 2 pm, from April to October, for guided tours in French. A reservation is required via their website or the Antibes Tourist Office will assist. It is advisable to drive to the location, though buses from Antibes do drive close by but not directly

to the Fondation. The tour will bring you to the studios used by the
artists where a number of paintings are hanging. The larger studio used
by Hartung still contains his paint brushes and multi-coloured spatters
on the walls. Usually an art expert is present during the group visit and
will tell visitors about the artists and their working methods. Use is
made of a video installation to display key paintings through the artists'
careers. There is a small shop selling postcards, books and graphic
works, the proceeds of which help defray the cost of maintaining
the beautiful Fondation.

Hans Hartung was born in Leipzig in 1904. From childhood he was
fascinated by lightning and thunder storms and this was a continuing
source of inspiration for him. He considered a religious career but an
instinctive love of drawing proved to be a more powerful impulse,
particularly after he saw the great painting *Braunschweig family group*
by Rembrandt which moved him greatly and decided him on a career
as a painter.

In Paris, poverty and loneliness were relieved by visits to museums
and by his meeting with Norwegian artist Anna-Eva Bergman whose
interest in abstract art coincided with his own. They married and
moved to the Spanish island of Minorca. In Minorca, they lived
frugally and painted to their hearts content until the onset of World
War Two when they came under suspicion as possible German spies.
Hartung was robustly opposed to the Nazis, and like de Staël, he
joined the French Foreign Legion to fight the Nazis during the
Second World War, during which he was shot in the leg, which
eventually led to its amputation. Although confined to a wheelchair, his
spirit was irrepressible. He and Bergman returned to live in Paris where
their reputations flourished in the 1950s and '60s as abstract art
became fashionable and sought after. Their prosperity enabled them
to move to the south of France where they purchased a site in an olive
grove on the outskirts of the Antibes where they supervised the
building of their dream house, Le Champ des Oliviers. It was based
on a simple white Minorcan fisherman's house in which they had once
lived. The 'white cube' concept was replicated a number of times around
a swimming pool that gave the two artists seclusion, perfection and
simplicity in which to pursue their creative goals.

Hartung was a very European abstract expressionist painter who graduated from grey and black compositions to coruscating fireworks of abstract painting in increasingly brilliant colours. As his style took flight, the avant-garde art market recognised him for the true original he was and in commercial galleries and at art auctions, his prices soared. In 1967, he was chosen to participate in the first ROSC International Art Exhibition in Dublin. Bergman painted in a similar vein, though her style was more restrained and less explosive.

Musée Peynet et du Dessin Humoristique can be found at place Nationale, Antibes. This small museum occupies a former school building in the prestigious city-centre square, where a weekly antiques flea market is held. Nearby is a tall stone historic column, and beside it is a small bronze sculpture of *Lovers*, cast in Paris, after drawn images of lovers by the cartoonist and popular image-maker Raymond Peynet (1908–99). This museum of popular and lightweight graphic and illustrational works is worth a brief visit for those with an interest in the genre.

The story of the minor draughtsman after whom the museum is named is of interest. Peynet was born in Paris and held various low-grade jobs before he succeeded in selling his folksy, whimsical drawings to leading magazines. He was a soldier in the Second World War and was captured by the Germans but escaped. He married Denise Damour in 1930. His sentimental drawings of two lovers became a popular brand, exploited commercially in different media. Japan, remarkably, has two museums dedicated to his work. The Peynets lived in Biot for a time and then moved to Antibes in 1976. The idea of a museum surfaced in the 1980s. It was inaugurated in 1995 with works by Peynet and other satirical cartoonists such as Daumier, Aldebert, Sennep and Meyer. The museum also contains gas masks, bayonets and helmets from the two World Wars. Peynet's oeuvre varied from political satire to book illustration and humorous caricature over a fifty-year period. France has celebrated his work by issuing a commemorative postage stamp on two occasions. The bronze sculpture of *Lovers* outside the museum is reminiscent of the sculpture of the Italian artist Giacomo Manzù (1908–91).

The **Cathedral of Our Lady of the Immaculate Conception** beside the Picasso Museum is worth a quick visit. It is built on the site of a Greek temple and is dedicated to Saints Sebastian, Réparate and Roch. It has pleasant glass windows featuring saints, and most notably *Christ in Majesty* wearing a cobalt blue garment which filters the bright Mediterranean light high over the altar. The church has a number of religious sculptures, of which the most memorable are the gilded image of Mary and the sorrowful carved *Head of the Crucified Christ*.

The **Musée d'Archéologie** at Bastion Saint-André in Antibes is well worth a quick stop to see the wealth of ancient artefacts that have been gathered there from many cultures. The building itself is dramatic. It is a single large space with a brick vaulted roof, built for military purposes on the orders of Napoleon, who resided nearby for some time. The museum contains Etruscan, Greek, Roman and Phoenician artefacts, many of them recovered from ancient shipwrecks by divers. There are many large shell-encrusted amphorae of Roman and Spanish origin; a fine display of Roman terracotta oil lamps, some of which bear relief sculptural images; a large mosaic floor fragment; attractive examples of Roman glass; and a variety of stone and metal funerary items.

A recent standout sculpture in Antibes is *La Nomade* by Spanish artist Jaume Plensa (*b.* 1955), who also created the celebratory light sculptures in place Masséna, Nice. The gigantic *La Nomade* figure at the port is made from cast iron letters welded together to allow light to filter through the seated form. The squatting figure, which dominates the port from the ramparts at Vauban, is an open form into which visitors can enter. It is eight metres high and gazes out over the blue-green waters of the Mediterranean Sea. Visitors will often encounter older sculptures dotted about, such as busts of Victor Hugo and Championnet, as they amble around the city. Both the museums and the joy of discovering these individual pieces ensure that Antibes is a must-see destination for lovers of art. An added attraction is the annual Antiques Fair held each summer near the port of Vauban. It attracts quality objets d'art, sculpture, and old and modern paintings from reputable art dealers throughout France. Keen art collectors can make enviable discoveries.

Saint-Paul de Vence is a must for all art lovers, as the area is rich in quality works of art. The number 400 bus takes you from Nice to the picturesque hilltop fortress in just under an hour. It was my custom to get off at the St-Paul stop and walk the few hundred metres of path by the little Chapelle Sainte-Clair. Then I decided to get off at the previous bus stop on the roundabout named for the Fondation Maeght, with the purpose of admiring the wonderful large rusted steel sculpture titled *Secret Point*, 2012, by French artist Jean-Claude Farhi (1940–2012), before proceeding uphill to the Fondation. It is just as well that I did, or I would have missed the impressive commercial Galerie Guy Pieters, which was located discreetly on chemin des Trions, from 2000. Sadly this ultra-modern and spacious gallery closed in 2015 and is a tremendous loss to the region. It was run by Guy and Linda Pieters, prominent modern-art dealers with galleries in the Belgian town of Knokke.

The **Fondation Maeght** is one of the artistic highlights of the whole region. There you will experience great modern sculpture and painting of the twentieth century. Marguerite and Aimé Maeght, who set it all up, are no longer alive, but it was run from the start as a very commercial business. Nowadays it is run by their daughter Isabelle. The admission fee is €15 for adults and there is no discount for senior citizens. There is an additional small fee if you wish to use video or take photographs. The expense is well worth it. I have witnessed visitors turning away at the gate because they considered it excessive but true art lovers must not be deterred.

The Maeghts were in the food business in Nice during times of scarcity in the Second World War; they became wealthy and began to collect contemporary art. They soon became major art dealers on the rue Teheran in Paris, representing most of the leading French artists of that time including Bonnard, Braque, Ubac, Arp, and expatriate artists Calder, Miró, Zadkine and Chillida. They lost their son Bernard, aged eleven, to leukaemia in 1953, and while in mourning discovered a dilapidated small chapel near their home at St-Paul de Vence which was dedicated to St Bernard. Their artist friends Braque and Léger are said to have advised them to use their wealth to restore the chapel in memory of their son. The idea blossomed after a visit to America where they visited the famed Barnes, Phillips and Guggenheim Collections. They soon decided to emulate them and create a unique French environment for contemporary art, where they could permanently display their impressive collection and where artists could create new works. Catalan architect Josep Lluís Sert was commissioned to design the complex, and he did so in partnership with leading artists such as Miró, Braque, Chagall, Ubac, Tal-Coat, Giacometti and others to bring about a unique artistic collaboration. The Fondation was established in 1964 and opened by André Malraux. It has gone from strength to strength since then, celebrating its fiftieth anniversary in 2014.

Over the years, it has staged many special temporary exhibitions as well as showing the permanent collection, and from time to time it borrows also from public and private collections. It encourages private patronage to add to the collection, which now contains over 6,000 works. In addition, it presents other artistic manifestations such as a performance by the Merce Cunningham Dance Company from the USA, music recitals by the cellist Mstislav Rostropovich and composer John Cage, among other celebrities. Irish artist Anne Madden shared an exhibition there in 1983 with Sam Francis, Louis Cane and Max Ernst, a most illustrious grouping. The Fondation also has an extensive art library and sells limited-edition prints, postcards, jewellery and scarves designed by artists.

The entrance pathway to the Fondation is flanked by major sculptures by artists such as Miró, Caro, Arp and Calder. There are even greater examples to the rear of the building complex, such as the majestic *La Touche* of 1963 in the labyrinth by Miró, and the sculpture court with twelve thin bronze figures by Alberto Giacometti, of which his two versions of *Walking Man* are most moving. Inside the building is a wonderful large painting of a blue, green and yellow landscape with nude female figures and children in the foreground by Pierre Bonnard whom the Maeghts considered to be the quintessential great artist of

their time. Finally, the little restored chapel in the grounds is a thing
of quiet, rare beauty. Braque (1927–2012) designed its gorgeous blue
and mauve stained-glass window with emblematic flying bird over the
altar place, and Raoul Ubac designed the more flamboyant window
titled *The Cross and the Rosary* on the facing wall. Ubac also carved
the understated, haunting small grey Stations of the Cross in slate.
It is a beautiful memorial to a boy who died far too young.

On the way out, there is a small café where weary visitors may drink
a coffee and reflect on the many treasures of modern art they have just
experienced.

It is only a short walk from the Maeght Foundation to the village
of St-Paul de Vence itself, which is full of art interest for tourists
and specialists alike. The robust tubular bronze female nude sculpture
Venus by Théo Tobiasse (1882–1963) stands impressively at the
entrance to the village. **Galerie Catherine Issert** is situated opposite
La Colombe d'Or Hotel and shows contemporary avant-garde art,
mostly abstract or non-representational. La Colombe d'Or art
collection is a treasure to be seen if at all possible. Hotel residents
and casual diners have free access to the art which graces the various
interior spaces, but it may also be possible to gain access if one uses
one's charm on the busy staff. The famous hotel, once known as 'The
Robinson', was bought and run by Paul and Titine Roux after the
First World War. Paul Roux began to paint in his spare time as a
young man and then progressed to a love of painting by contemporary
masters. When he was not at the hotel, he was out painting in the

Various eminent artworks can be seen throughout La Colombe d'Or Hotel

Le Carré d'Agneau de Sisteron
avec sa garniture de légumes

Civet de Lapin du Facteur

Rognons à la Provençale

Poussin à la Chipolata

Fricassée de Volaille
et aux Morilles

Haricots Verts sautés au Beurre

Salade

landscape with brushes and easel, and he soon became acquainted with professional painters in the vicinity such as Derain, Matisse, Picasso, Rouault, Léger, Bonnard and others who were relatively unknown then but are world-famous today. Legend has it that he fed the impoverished artists in exchange for good examples of their paintings. Whatever the reality was, he seems to have had rare good judgement, as the collection that remains today to honour his memory is world-class. It contains so many lovely items that I am hard-pressed to mention favourites. A painting of a red lobster by Braque must be one. The little head of a woman by Rouault is another, and there is a stunning colourful abstract by the Russian-born Sonia Delaunay-Terk. There is a wonderful large red, black and white painted steel *Mobile* by Alexander Calder near the swimming pool and an equally delightful smaller one in red and black hanging indoors. Inside the front door is a small still life by Paul Roux himself, which proves that the former proprietor was more than just competent as an artist: it holds up well to the works of the professionals. The hotel obviously keeps up to date as a work on paper, dated 1994, by Irish-American Sean Scully (*b.* 1945), hangs in one of the relaxing rooms. Members of the Roux family still manage the business. The hotel is famed for the excellence of its food and you need to book well in advance to secure a reservation.

St-Paul de Vence has commercial art galleries to suit most tastes – too many to list here. I invariably visit **Galerie Golconda** near the Grande Fontaine in the middle of the hilly main street. It has a fine collection of Han dynasty Chinese ceramic and Etruscan artefacts, as well as south-east Asian bronzes and objets d'art. The Han dynasty in China lasted from 206 BC to AD 220, so the artefacts that date from that period are approximately 2,000 years old. The thousands of beautiful small clay sculptures of animals and humans that were excavated from the ancient tombs in many provinces in the early twentieth century were originally tomb furnishings, buried with important dignitaries, to help them in the afterlife. They were made from red or grey clay and fired in kilns with a lead-glaze which was frequently green, though long burial in the tombs often resulted in interesting colour changes. For two or three decades the Chinese authorities allowed their export without restriction, and European and American museums and astute traders and collectors avidly collected them. It was really only after the

discovery, decades later, of the huge army of life-size ceramic warriors at the massive T'ang tombs at Xian that their export was seriously prohibited. Galerie Golconda is fortunate to have a good selection of functional pottery and clay animals for sale from the Han period, and sometimes exquisite small earthenware horses and camels with attractive green and brown glazes from the later T'ang dynasty (AD 618–906). They don't come cheap any more, but they are rather beautiful art objects to modern eyes, despite their anonymity. The ancient fountain on the main street is now an official historic monument, as are a number of other buildings in the town centre.

The **Galerie le Capricorne** shows works by Warhol, Picasso, Matisse, Chagall and Arman. In a very small cemetery outside the corner of the ramparts, the artist Marc Chagall is buried. Not far away is the Église, also a historic monument, dating from the thirteenth to the

Femme à l'Ombrelle 1913 Robert Delaunay Oil on board

eighteenth century. Among its ancient religious paintings, pride of place is granted to a statue of the Virgin Mary. The nearby Donjon, dating from the twelfth century, is now also a historic monument. So is the simple little **Chapelle des Pénitents Blancs**, where mass is no longer regularly celebrated but which was sensitively redecorated by the Belgian artist Jean-Michel Folon (1934–2005), who resided here for many years. He painted the walls in pastel shades with quiet images of hands releasing birds to suggest calm, peace and happiness. Over the altar he created an attractive landscape, or rather townscape, of St-Paul de Vence in mosaic, preceded by a stone sculpture of a standing man wearing a hat and feeding the birds. Presumably this is the artist's vision of St Francis communing with nature. There is another sculpture of a large bronze hand on which stands a little man: it is surely a symbol of humankind and its Creator. The whole ensemble is nicely balanced by the modern stained-glass windows with pale images of flowers and buds, all designed by Folon, who died just before his visionary redecoration was completed. It gives me a new respect for an artist whom I previously considered a rather stolid academic sculptor.

The **Church of the Conversion of Saint Paul** at the summit is handsomely furnished with ancient religious paintings, including an image of Saint Catherine of Alexandria, said to have been painted in part by the great Venetian master Tintoretto (1518–94). It is a baroque experience to be enjoyed, if the visitor is not already exhausted by the abundance of things to be experienced.

The final commercial art gallery recommended to visitors is **Galerie l'Art Vivant**, which shows works by Hartung, Miró, Chillida and Del Re. It also offers scarves, books and jewellery for sale. A visit to the town of Vence itself, a few kilometres away, might best be put off for another day. Treat yourself instead to a sumptuous meal at the fabulous La Colombe d'Or Hotel outdoor restaurant, where the food and wine are delicious, and though it will set you back a goodly sum, it will be an experience to remember.

Vence, like other towns in the region, was a Ligurian settlement before the arrival of the Romans, who occupied it for a time. It is a short three-kilometre journey from St-Paul by bus or car. The main art attractions are the **Chapelle du Rosaire** and **Espace Matisse**, the **Fondation Émile Hugues**, the **Chapelle des Pénitents Blancs**, a number of commercial art galleries, and the ancient cathedral in the old town.

The **Chapelle du Rosaire**, otherwise known as the **Matisse Chapel**, was built for the Dominican nuns and is a ten-minute walk from the bus terminal. You must cross a narrow bridge over a deep gorge on the route signposted to Gattières, then follow a pot-holed footpath until you eventually arrive at the modest building that was transformed by Matisse after the Second World War. The story behind it is well known. Matisse refused to leave his home and studio in Cimiez, Nice at the start of the war, as he was convalescing after a serious operation. He was attended constantly by his assistant, Lydia Delectorskaya, but he needed a night nurse as well. He hired a young woman, Monique Bourgeois, who answered an advertisement for a 'young and pretty' attendant. She is reputed to have modelled for him as well as attending to his medical needs. Later, she became a Dominican nun and was sent to live in a convent at Vence just opposite a villa taken later by Matisse to wait out the end of the war, which was endangering his abode at Nice. The nuns were using an unsatisfactory former garage space as a chapel and dreamed of raising money to build a new one. Monique, now called Soeur Jacques-Marie, showed the artist a design for a stained-glass window for the old chapel for which he agreed to pay. An idea then began to form in Matisse's head, culminating in a decision to design a new chapel for the nuns. It took his entire time from 1946 to 1951 to bring this dream to realisation. Matisse, the master, insisted on designing everything to do with the chapel, from the long, thin

Matisse Chapel (stained glass detail)

Entrance to Matisse Chapel

altar candlesticks inspired by an anemone flower, to the colourful vestments to be worn by the priests celebrating mass in the new chapel. Matisse was in his eighties and wheelchair-bound, but he could not be restrained from attending to every aspect of the creation. The result was a little masterpiece of modern religious art.

Matisse used long poles to hold his brushes while drawing the stark minimal black human images on the cool white walls, lined with smooth faience tiles from Vallauris. One wall to the right of the altar is covered from floor to ceiling with an image of *St Dominic Holding a Bible*. Another wall, titled *Ave*, contains cloud-forms and a very simplified outline drawing of the *Virgin and Child*, with the infant's arms extended to form the sign of the cross. On the back wall of the little chapel, Matisse ingeniously concentrated all fourteen images of the Stations of the Cross, drawn in a stark ultra-modern representational conception.

Nearby is a beautifully pierced and decorated door through which the nuns may enter the chapel to kneel in the soberly designed brown seating area. Colour floods into the magical space through a series of scintillating modern stained-glass windows, designed by the artist to make the most of the sun's traverse across the sky. Using blue, yellow and green, Matisse stayed with abstraction for all of the windows, with the exception of the wonderful *Tree of Life* window over the modest stone altar, which glows with frond shapes developed from his cut-out series that had begun in his Regina studio in Cimiez a few years earlier. Paul Bony helped Matisse to fabricate the stained-glass windows for the chapel. He was a famous glass artisan who helped many artists in the twentieth century to realise their designs.

Experiencing the Matisse Chapel is profoundly moving. Matisse considered it his masterpiece. The nuns charge €6 for admission and have a little shop in which preparatory drawings are exhibited as well as Matisse's unique liturgical vestments. The postcards are relatively dear, but it is all in a good cause as the nuns probably need the revenue for the upkeep of the chapel and convent. Tourists of all denominations flock to this religious centre that exudes a palpable aura of spirituality.

Check the opening hours at a tourist office as they vary depending on the day and time of year. As you walk back from the Matisse Chapel towards the old town, you will encounter the **Roman Washhouse**, now a protected building, and soon after that the Chapelle des Pénitents Blancs, which is no longer in use for religious purposes but which occasionally hosts art exhibitions. Beside it is a relief portrait plaque to the poet Frédéric Mistral (1830–1914) by Victor Marea. Further down the ancient street leading to the old quarter are a number of small commercial art galleries. My favourite to visit is **Galerie Chave** at 13, rue Henri Isnard, which exhibits paintings, drawings and etchings by artists of reputation including Max Ernst, Henri Michaux and Kim En Joong.

There is a wonderful view over the deep gorge and towards the mountains from the boulevard Fernand Moutet. Beside it is **Fondation Émile Hugues**, which exhibits modern art from the region, featuring artists such as Claude Viallat and others. There is an admission charge of €7, and it includes an excellent shop selling postcards and souvenirs. The Fondation now occupies what was once La Château de Villeneuve on the west rampart of this historic town. The castle was then the residence of the Villeneuve family, who were the aristocratic lords of Vence until the French Revolution in 1789.

There is much else to see in this charming old town. An attractive bronze cubist sculpture of a young woman, entitled *La Vençoise*, stands on a plinth at place Clemenceau outside the Hôtel de Ville. Nearby is the ancient cathedral, a historic building with a particularly dark interior though full of painting and sculptural treasures, including a recent mosaic by Marc Chagall, who lived in the vicinity. The cathedral has some multicoloured stained-glass windows that may not be as old as the main fabric of the splendid, ancient rococo building.

Nearby is the **Musée Provençal** for those who still wish to explore the history of this ancient settlement from pre-Roman times. The flea market is held in place Clemenceau on Wednesdays. Apart from art, Vence is a thriving centre with many interesting shops and lots of restaurants serving regional dishes and wines.

The city of Cannes is still regarded as the most fashionable resort on the French Riviera, a place where the rich and famous come to dine and party. The annual Cannes Film Festival takes place over twelve days in May and draws thousands of visitors from all over the world. Rents and hotel prices peak during that period. The glittering city has enviable sandy beaches and a most pretty harbour for luxury yachts, overlooked by the old quarter of Le Suquet with its high, square, eleventh-century watchtower, the Tour de Mont Chevalier, and the Musée de la Castre nearby. The long promenade known as La Croisette is lined with magnificent hotel buildings and luxury shops. It got its name from a little cross which used to stand on the tip of the Pointe de la Croisette where tourists embark for the islands of Lérins. The city itself got its name from the sugarcane fields which surrounded the city in the nineteenth century. In 1834 an English aristocrat, Lord Brougham, and his tubercular daughter were visiting what was then a mere village of a few thousand people. They were confined there when a cholera epidemic in France led to the border with Italian Savoy being closed. They stayed at the only hotel in the village. The lord was so taken by the region's benign climate and

Mural at Cannes bus station

natural beauty that he decided to have a luxury villa built there and to spend his winters in Cannes henceforth. It started a fashion that other British nationals were to follow. He is commemorated today by an impressive stone statue dated 1878 on a high pedestal in front of a shallow pool facing the port, in an area that has been massively developed since his time.

Cannes may not have the historical artistic riches of Nice, but it is growing more interesting year by year for art lovers as it recognises the huge tourist potential of art and art exhibitions. We will start with Le Cannet, a hilly suburb near where the great modern French painter Pierre Bonnard (1867–1947) spent some of his most fruitful days with his model and eventual wife, Marthe de Méligny, née Maria Boursin.

L'Amandier 1930 Pierre Bonnard Oil on canvas

They were a reclusive couple, living simply and shunning excess. Their daily lives were the subject of his art. He was friendly with fellow artists Maurice Denis (1870–1943) and Paul Sérusier (1864–1927) and considered himself a disciple of the post-impressionist Paul Gauguin (1848–1903). Bonnard was part of a group of contemporaries, including Édouard Vuillard (1868–1940), who were known as Les Nabis, 'The Prophets'. They proposed to reinvent modern painting. Bonnard drew and painted Marthe again and again. She was slight and delicate and the ideal model for the artist. He painted many nude versions of her in sensuous colours over the years, making sure to exclude her face, as she was sensitive to recognition. The artist also had a strong attachment to nature, and painted many beautiful pictures of Le Cannet and its environs. Gardens and still life compositions were also subjects for his painting, and he turned to self-portraits in old age after his wife died. His sculptor friend Aristide Maillol (1861–1944) then lent him his partner and model, voluptuous Dina Vierny, to inspire Bonnard to return to figurative painting. He did so, by asking her to move about the studio and not to take up a fixed pose. Some of his most beautiful paintings of garden scenes were made in his last year, when he chose an almond tree in full blossom as the subject of lyrical, explosive expressions of beauty and sadness. The Tate Gallery in London and the Museum of Modern Art, New York held a wonderful posthumous retrospective exhibition in 1998, which included many of these ravishing late paintings. Le Cannet has now done him the honour of building an impressive new museum on the main street of the suburb in his memory.

The easiest way to get to the **Musée Bonnard** on boulevard Sadi Carnot is to take the number 1 bus from the bus station in Cannes. The museum is really a modern addition to an impressive old building, **l'Hôtel Saint-Vianney**, *c.*1920, which stands in front of the Church of Saint Philomena. The architects of the new museum were Frédéric Ferrero and Sylvie Rossi from Vence, and it was inaugurated on 25 June 2011 by the mayor of Le Cannet in the presence of Frédéric Mitterrand, French Minister of Culture and Communications. Since the new museum opened it has staged a number of impressive exhibitions, borrowing suitable works from other museums and

private collectors. One year, it celebrated the life of socialite Misia Sert, the wife of Catalan architect Josep Lluís Sert who designed the Maeght Fondation at Saint-Paul de Vence. She was a pianist and an extrovert beauty who was known to and painted by many of the leading French artists of her time.

In 2014 the theme of the exhibition was *Les Belles Endormies* (The Sleeping Beauties) and it contained masterly works by Bonnard and his friends and contemporaries, including Sérusier, Matisse, Manguin, Lombard, Renoir, Vallotton, Maillol, Delvaux, Picasso, Brancusi, Balthus, Tal-Coat and Van Dongen. Among the standouts were the gorgeous little polished bronze head of the *Muse Endormie* of 1910 by Constantin Brancusi (1876–1957), lent by the Pompidou Museum in Paris, and *L'Amandier,* the flowering almond tree of 1930 by Bonnard, donated by Fondation Meyer in 2014. Aimé Maeght considered Bonnard the outstanding artist of his time, *primus inter pares*. Visitors to Cannes should not miss this new avant-garde museum.

Villa Domergue on the outskirts of Cannes is a hidden treasure. The Art déco house and gardens were designed by artists Jean–Gabriel and Odette Domergue in the 1920s. They later bequeathed it to the city and it now hosts the annual Cannes Film Festival jury. Each year it also holds a major art exhibition and in

Nu devant profil 1917 Pierre Bonnard Oil on canvas

2015 it featured an exquisite collection of drawings by Paul Cézanne from private and public collections. The villa is open to the public from July to September. It is best approached by taxi from the city centre, though the number 6 or number 7 bus will drop you within a 10-minute walk of the villa.

The **Musée de la Castre** in Cannes is up on the hill in the old town, looking down on the new. It is a must-visit venue for lovers of primitive and ethnic art, gathered from the four corners of the world by intrepid travellers and collectors. The major donor was a Dutch baron named Tinco Martinus Lycklama à Nijeholt, who donated his fascinating collection in 1873, and it was subsequently added to by donations from French artistic hunter-gatherers.

The museum was established in 1877 and has an old-fashioned feel to it, but don't be put off by that. It has one of the best collections of Oceanic, Asian, South American and African ethnic art that I have encountered anywhere in the world, as well as an enormous collection of antique musical instruments. Among the highlights are a blazingly coloured textile of a fierce face from Tibet (a protector of religion), and a wonderful terracotta stylised female ceramic figure from the Chancay Culture in Peru (twelfth to fifteenth century). There are some amazing Tiki-poteau carved wooden idols from the Marquesas Islands, one of which featured on a poster throughout Cannes advertising the 'Expressive Primitive as Inspiration' exhibition that showed in 2014 at three locations. There are cases full of Etruscan, Greek and Oriental small bronzes and ceramics, as well as Egyptian sarcophagi and many other amazing artistic and religious objects from the wide world of the past.

The museum also contains a paintings section, particularly landscape and marine paintings of the Côte d'Azur in the nineteenth century by artists such as Contini (1827–92), H.-J. Harpignies (1819–1916), Felix Ziem (1821–1911), Alexis Mossa (1844–1926), and other lesser-known artists. They reveal how much the environs of Cannes have changed in a little over a century.

Finally, there is a fascinating collection of Persian weapons and
armour and a group of Middle-Eastern eighteenth- and nineteenth-
century paintings of courtesans and courtyard scenes by unknown
artists during the reign of the Qajars from Persia. The subtly painted
canvases differ in technique from Western paintings and reveal to
conservators that the Persians used gold paint made from actual
gold dust to repair their paintings when they suffered damage over
the years.

The tall **Watchtower** beside the Castre Museum dates from the
eleventh century and is open to visitors brave enough to mount the
109 steps which lead to the top of the lookout tower. Those who do
will be rewarded with stunning panoramic views of the city, the sea
and the coastline as far up as Nice and way out beyond the Lérins
islands. Historically, watchmen could signal from its top to warn other
points on the coast of an impending Saracen invasion. Centuries later,
the tower became a prison for a time. Outside of the museum there is
a bronze portrait of Fr Bellini (1904–89) mounted on a stone plinth,
describing him as an architect, artist and painter. He must have been
intimately concerned with the fabric of the museum to deserve such
a fine memorial.

The nearby **Église de Suquet** is a splendid, substantial Catholic
church building dedicated to Saint Rita. It has old religious paintings
still in situ and gilded statues of the Virgin Mary with infant Jesus.
The bare ceiling suggests previous damage and recent repair, as one
vaulted area is covered with frescoes and contains ancient ecclesiastical
treasures from the past. One unusual feature of this church is a display
case containing many small, colourful Provençal dolls of the past, and
typical of the region and similar to those seen in Cagnes-sur-Mer.

Outside of the church, on a high vantage point overlooking the city,
is an impressive carved sandstone sculpture of *The Virgin with Infant
Jesus* of 1948 by artist Emile Patras. Steep steps lead down to the
newer city at sea level from this high point.

The next major art exhibition space, and an artistic highlight of the city, is the **Centre d'Art la Malmaison** on boulevard de la Croisette. For a start, it is a very beautiful period building, now under municipal jurisdiction. It displays a few special exhibitions of the highest quality each year, with a substantial charge for admission, but it is well worth a visit. It used to close for lunch but no longer does, which is a boon for visitors. It also sells catalogues, art postcards and other souvenirs. Recent years have seen outstanding exhibitions here, featuring Russian artists in France in the twentieth century, the drawings of Picasso from family collections, graphic works by Georges Braque, a retrospective exhibition of the talented French artist Szczęsny, and in 2014 the stunning 'From Primitive Expression to Inspired Vision', featuring outstanding examples of primitive art alongside sculptures, drawings, prints and paintings by more than ninety famous modern artists who were influenced by ethnic art. The modern artists included Warhol, Picasso, Miró, Man Ray, Braque, Calder, Giacometti, Cesár, Max Ernst, Léger, Niki de Saint Phalle, Tinguely, Penck and many others. It complemented the exhibition at the Musée de la Castre and the third related exhibition at the Musée de la Mer on a nearby Lérins island. Outside of La Malmaison in the summer of 2014 stood three large polychromed bronze sculptures of Venus by the American artist Jim Dine, who was born in 1935. They were lent, courtesy of the Pieters Gallery which was then in St-Paul de Vence, and no doubt were for sale at commanding prices. In 2015 the Sapone Gallery in Nice lent 200 choice drawings and paintings by the Italian-born artist Alberto Agnelli (1888–1971) who lived for a time in Vallauris. The exhibition was a delightful revelation.

Cannes is definitely the playground of Europe. One sees more Rolls Royces here than anywhere else on the Riviera. It has also become a centre for the sale of expensive art and art-related objects. In summer 2014, in the grounds of the Grand Hotel, a large temporary tent exhibition space was installed featuring gorgeous carpets, glass objects, and sculpture reproductions of works of art by the master Georges Braque for sale, all described as Le Maître Artisan. I did not dare to enquire about prices, though I learned later that they started at €20,000 and went up to €1,000,000. The ceramics were fabricated at nearby Vallauris.

Throughout Cannes one encounters many public sculptures as one strolls about the palm-lined promenade. There are also many commercial art galleries along the central rue d'Antibes or on side streets off it. There are too many to list individually, so I will mention some that are particularly worthy of a visit.

Galerie Gantois on rue d'Antibes shows colourful contemporary paintings and sculpture by local artists, but also lithographs by Miró. **Galerie de Cannes**, also on rue d'Antibes, displays a wide variety of art and has an international clientele. **Galerie Hurtebize**, on boulevard de La Croissette, shows paintings by Souverbie, Buffet and others. **Galerie Dansleciel**, on rue Commandant Vidal, shows contemporary, mostly abstract avant-garde art. It has a sister gallery in Mougins.

In summer 2014 a large exhibition of modern art from Azerbaijan took place at the **Gare Maritime** building on the seafront. At the entrance to this building visitors can't fail to notice an attractive ceramic frieze mounted on the wall by artist Roger Capron in 1957. Dotted about the promenade are portrait busts of eminent persons and bronzes of animals and Venuses of varying quality. It is no surprise, therefore, to come across a bronze sculpture, *Homage to the Cinema*, featuring a movie camera swathed in reels of film by Max Cartier (*b.* 1935) near the Conference Centre. I prefer, however, the impressive large bronze memorial group of soldiers with angel on a high plinth outside the **Hôtel de Ville** near the old town. It salutes and remembers all those who fought for France in the two World Wars, in Europe, Africa and the Orient. Gazing at it makes one reflect on the meaning of life and how precious it is, and how terrible are the results of war. It is a fitting conclusion to a tour of art manifestations in glamorous Cannes.

Villefranche is a most picturesque town just behind the headland after Nice. It has a world-famous deep-water harbour that has attracted boats and sailors from time immemorial. It still does so, often giving anchorage to two massive cruise liners at a time. Many artists have visited the beauty spot to draw and paint there. Nathaniel Hone the Second, RHA (1831–1917) an important Irish Barbizon-trained painter of the nineteenth century, sailed into the harbour on at least one occasion and made numerous quick pencil drawings of fishermen at their nets. These impressions, together with sketchbooks full of lightning-quick watercolours, were the material from which he later made some of his best oil paintings in his studio in Malahide, County Dublin. After his death in 1917, his widow donated a large collection of his paintings and sketchbooks to the National Gallery of Ireland.

Villefranche can be reached fairly quickly by boarding the number 100 bus near the Nice Museum of Modern and Contemporary Art, or by train from the Gare Centrale in Nice. The bus journey offers spectacular sea views. One alights at Octroi bus stop to begin the art exploration, and there is plenty to see for a whole day. Visitors should be aware of the widespread practice in this town of closing at lunchtime for up to three hours during the summer season. The tourist office at Octroi park provides a map of the hilly town and brochures detailing the museums and cultural highlights therein.

Octroi Park contains three sculptures worthy of attention. The central sandstone War Memorial on a high plinth, by artist M. Le Blanc, pays tribute to the many local inhabitants who lost their lives in the service of France during the two World Wars. It comprises an upright column with a starry sphere at its apex. At its base is a bronze cock standing proudly on the arms and flags of the fallen. Plaques detail the names and ages of those who died. Sadly, most were in their twenties. The monument was sculpted in Nice in 1925 and paid for by public subscription.

The memorial is flanked by two sensuous *Female Nude* stone carvings by the most prominent local sculptor, Antoniucci Voltigerno, known as Volti, who was born in Albano, Italy, in 1915 and died in Paris in 1989. Throughout his life Volti was inspired by the beauty of the female form, and he celebrated it in drawings, modelling and carving. Only seldom did he model the male form. The two well-rounded sculptures on plinths in the garden at Octroi are among his best works. Both females are seated, one with arms akimbo and the other with arms crossed.

The **Citadelle** is an imposing fortress built in 1557 on the orders of Emmanuel-Philibert of Savoy to defend the town against attacks. It was restored in 1981 and now houses the **Hôtel de Ville** (Town Hall) and four small artistic and cultural museums. Entry is free to all four museums. The **Volti Museum** nestles at the base of the Bastion La Turbie of the citadel and the bronze and plaster casts are interestingly sited in both tunnel-like spaces and outdoor garden openings. One is struck immediately by the skill and power of Volti. He was a formidable three-dimensional artist who reminds me very much of his contemporary, the great English sculptor Henry Moore. The museum brochure claims him to be in the company of eminent twentieth-century French sculptors such as Rodin, Maillol and Bourdelle. Volti was not as great a draughtsman as Henry Moore, nor had he Moore's powers of creative imagination, but he was a popular, skilful practitioner who made some wonderful reclining figures – like

Moore's but more traditional in form, and without the see-through holes and dynamic distortions typical of the English master. One of Volti's favourite themes was maternity. His bronze cast of a pregnant woman with full breasts and bulging stomach attests to this, and stands impressively outside the entrance to the museum. Beside it is yet another of his beautiful well-rounded stone nude females, this time seated on a low stone wall in the foreground. A magnificent bronze of a young female, with an attractive

dark green patina, also stands on a plinth in front of the Town Hall. Here, she is almost completely and unashamedly naked, with a drape falling to the ground beneath her knees. It is an exceptional work of art. Beside it there is a mosaic depiction of a reclining female nude, by an unspecified artist, after a work by Volti.

One of the most beautiful Volti works in the museum is his carved maquette for *The Three Graces*. The large stone sculpture, for which this must have been the study, is in the middle of a fountain near the Méridien Hotel in Nice. Three beautiful young women embrace each other and compete for the prize of the gods. A rare exception to his norm is the most moving sculpture of the *Christian Martyr*, who kneels in resignation and peace with his faith before his execution. This work won the artist the 2nd Prix de Rome in 1936, when he was only twenty-one years old. Sadly, he lost the use of his arm half a century year later, in 1985, and could no longer sculpt. Yet he persisted to draw the female form for as long as pain and suffering could allow. He died in Paris in 1989, some five years after the better-known Henry Moore. A retrospective exhibition of his sculptures was held in China and Villefranche in 2015 to celebrate the centenary of his birth.

The **Goetz-Boumeester Museum** is tucked away in the fortress of the citadel and is worth a quick visit, though both artists after whom the museum is named are of relatively minor stature. Some fifty works by

Christine Boumeester and an equivalent number by her husband, Henri
Goetz, were donated to the town of Villefranche-sur-Mer along with
several small works of art they received as gifts from more famous
contemporaries. They lived locally on rue Baron de Brès. Many
photographs show that they were on friendly terms with Picasso, Picabia,
Miró, Zao Wu Ki, Hartung, Ubac and Vieira de Silva. Boumeester was
born in Djakarta, Indonesia in 1904, of Dutch stock, and died in Paris in
1971. She started out as an academic artist with an obvious facility to draw
and use watercolours. She developed to become an abstract artist mainly
influenced by Hans Hartung. Henri Goetz was born in the USA in 1909
and died in 1989, outliving Christine by eighteen years. He collected
African carvings and was something of a surrealist. His oil painting *Hélice
Chagrinée*, 1947, is impressive, while his self-portrait of 1935 reveals a face
of strong resolute character. His surrealist portrait of Christine in 1937
shows her to have been an attractive woman. He is credited with inventing
the technique of carborundum printmaking which is proving to be a
popular form of graphic art making.

The **Roux Collection** is the third little museum in the citadel. It comprises
several hundred ceramic figurines of men and women in their colourful
costumes down through the ages. Soldiers, sailors, dancers, courtiers, kings
and princes, archers and tyrants, as well as ancient castles and dungeons, are
all skilfully modelled and polychromed to a fascinating high standard, and
the whole exhibition is imaginatively displayed. It might be of particular
interest to children. No information is provided on how the collection was
formed or by whom it was donated.

The **Memorial Hall of the 24th Battalion of the Alpine Hunters** is the
fourth little museum in the citadel complex. From 1876 to 1939 this
battalion, the successor to the battalion of foot soldiers under Napoleon III,
was the last army corps to occupy the citadel monument. Souvenirs of
the battalion are on display in the hall – badges, banners, photographs,
etchings, and so on. There is a video showing soldiers marching to
regimental music.

The **Chapelle Saint-Elme** in the complex has reconstructions of trench
warfare during the First World War, and souvenirs and copies of memorials

to the many soldiers who died for France. It is a sobering experience to enter that space through reproduction torn sackcloth, and listen to the nostalgic and sad songs of wartime.

Outside there is a bronze bust of Jean Moulin, who was a leader in the French Resistance during the Second World War. It stands on a plinth between two massive rusting cannons, known in England as 'pounders', pointing out to the bay. Near at hand, in a little courtyard, is a life-size sculpture made of stones and rusty iron by Max Cartier, whose major work in this genre stands on the roundabout at Nice airport. It may appeal to some, but it is too crude for my taste.

Inside the entrance gate to the **Ancient Fort of St-Elme** is a small informative display room containing ancient Etruscan, Greek and Roman artefacts recently recovered from the seabed of the bay by expert divers. The items mostly date from the sixteenth to the eighteenth centuries, during which many powerful galleys came to anchor in the harbour. The items are mostly ceramic bowls and plates originating in Provence, Spain and the great cities of Italy. Beside them is a dredged up wreck of a small galley still laden with broken pots and shards. This more or less completes the artistic experience in the massive citadel. It is good to see it still in use and welcoming visitors.

St Peter's Chapel is a pretty little 600-year-old Romanesque-style chapel on the quai Courbet at the water's edge. It is a delightful surprise, wonderfully decorated by Jean Cocteau, and well worth a visit. Cocteau was something of an enigma from the north of France. He was an unhappy child at school, most probably because of the suicide of his father when he was quite young. He developed into a celebrated artist, turning his hand to poetry, painting, drawing, film-making and involvement in music and dance through writing librettos for the Ballet Russe in Monte Carlo. He made the acquaintance of many celebrities, including Picasso and Matisse, and vied with them for artistic recognition, though his genuine drawing talent was of a much lesser order than theirs. He came to the south of France and made friends with the wealthy Weisweiller family who resided in a luxurious villa near Villefranche. He was eventually invited to stay with that family at no personal expense for a few years, and it was during this period that he decorated the little Fishermen's Chapel from October 1956 to July 1957. The result is a triumph. The once derelict building used by the local fishermen to store nets and floats has been transformed through the artist's creative imagination into a jewel of draughtsmanship and pale pastel colouring. The municipal authorities who at first resisted the idea were delighted with the ultimate result, which draws many tourists to visit the area. It is likely that Cocteau first got the idea to decorate a chapel twenty years earlier when he saw Matisse's brilliant decoration of the Dominican Chapel in Vence.

Cocteau frescoed the ceiling with a lattice-work of images of fishermen's nets. He covered the walls with his characteristic drawing technique, but on a larger scale than before, using the theme of Saint Peter in various aspects of his life. One panel pays homage to the gypsies of Saintes-Maries-de-la-Mer. It contains a young flamenco dancer and a guitarist with two young women gazing over a balustrade. Cocteau cleverly made these women into likenesses of his patrons, Francine Weisweiller and her daughter Carole, who bankrolled the undertaking.

Another panel pays homage to the girls of Villefranche dressed in their traditional regional costumes. A third panel has Saint Peter being handed over to the soldiers, weeping beside a cock, recalling that Jesus predicted he would deny Him three times as the cock crows. A fourth panel depicts St Peter sleeping chained between two soldiers. He had been imprisoned by King Herod but is helped by an angel.

The final panel over the little altar is a tour-de-force of draughtsmanship. Saint Peter walks on water, helped by Christ, who gives his blessing. The observing fishermen and even the fishes of the sea themselves are amazed at the miraculous sight. Angels and figures holding tridents people the background. The whole effect is rather glorious, perhaps Cocteau's masterpiece, and superior to his various efforts elsewhere. Cocteau also decorated the Weisweiller Villa, which is still in private ownership but may be viewed by prior appointment.

The artist used charcoal and chalk with pale paint to get his effects, and the drawings were fixed with a mixture prepared from paraffin oil. There are long relief paintings on either side of the church door to complete the ensemble. A good selection of postcards is available to purchase as souvenirs. The attendant told me that mass is still celebrated in the church once a year on 29 June, mainly for the benefit of local fishermen.

A bronze portrait bust of Jean Cocteau can be seen on a plinth at the seafront and near his little church in the Port de la Santé. It was cast in 1989 and is by the artist Cyril de la Patellière. It is a very good likeness of the multi-talented, tempestuous artist. His stylish signature is reproduced on the stone plinth underneath, together with one of his single characteristic stars.

The old town of Villefranche has a few other features worth seeing. The first is the fourteenth-century **rue Obscure**, a street now designated a historic monument. It runs by the ramparts and was once a secret passageway for military movements before being covered over. **St Michel's Church** in the heart of the old town, also classified as a historic monument, is a splendid building of the eighteenth century in the baroque style. It features statues of St Roch, St Rita and St Francis of Assisi, and a famous carving of a recumbent Christ by an anonymous galley slave, which was absent undergoing conservation in 2014. The ceiling is not frescoed but the chapel has an elaborate oil painting of St Michael spearing the damned (the devil). St Michael is the patron saint of both the town and the church.

Saint Elizabeth's Chapel on the rue de l'Église is now deconsecrated and is in occasional use as a temporary art exhibition space. It dates from the sixteenth century. It offers no information about opening times, but the tourist office says it is hired from time to time by individual artists. Several artists' ateliers are open to the public on adjoining small side streets.

This completes the artistic survey of beautiful Villefranche-sur-Mer, which is well worth a full day's visit. Visitors can enjoy a glass or two of the local wine to accompany a tasty lunch at one of the many excellent restaurants by the seashore. As is the case all along the Côte d'Azur, the views of mountain and sea are breathtaking and in Villefranche the higher up the hill the more spectacular the panorama.

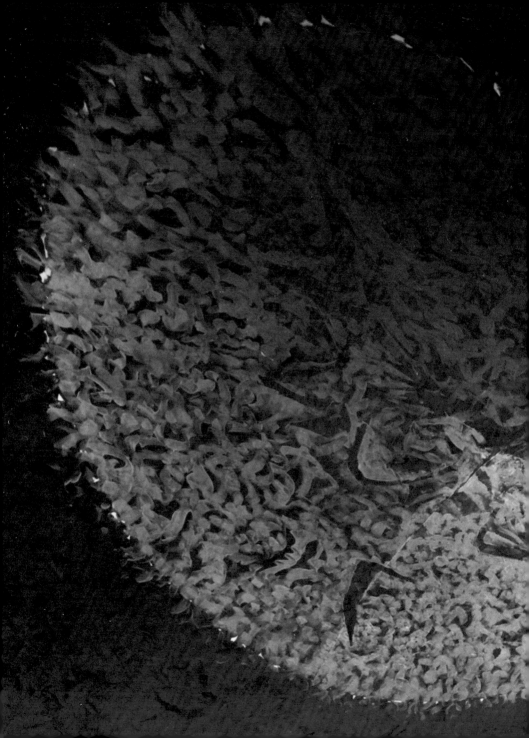

Carros Village and Le Broc

I would recommend a journey up to these lovely mountain villages only if you are a dedicated art explorer with plenty of time to spare, and preferably driving a car. There is not much modern art to see there, and the bus service entails long delays. I have visited, by car and bus, and each time enjoyed the experience, as the views of land and sea from the Alpes-Maritimes are truly exhilarating. Don't get confused between Carros and the place to aim for, the delightful Carros Village, a further three or four kilometres up the hill. If you take the number 500 bus from beside the **Galerie Lafayette** in Nice, you may have to disembark at Carros – not all of the buses continue up to the village, though the tourist office in Nice may not tell you that. Should that be your misfortune, you may have to wait for quite some time for a smaller 701a bus, which travels irregularly from La Marida through Carros Village and Le Broc to Bouyon. Alternatively, you could walk up the long, winding road through the wooded landscape to the ancient village on the hill and enjoy birdsong and the perfumed scents of the mountain flora along the way.

The ancient and tiny village of Carros stands more than 300 metres over the winding river Var and is particularly pretty and compact. The local tourist office is situated in the **Barbary Villa**, named after a former mayor of the village. It also acts as a small exhibition space for traditional local costumes and artefacts of the region, some of which are for sale, and it dispenses teas, coffees and cold drinks at modest prices. The village boasts a single restaurant, some artists' ateliers, and a seventeenth-century church which was built and completed by the princely de Blacas family in 1664 but damaged by an earthquake in 1887, and no longer open to the public on a regular basis. But the crowning glory of this twelfth-century village, built on a more ancient site once occupied by the Romans, is the thirteenth-century château, which has been restored and converted in recent times to become the **Centre International d'Art Contemporain (CIAC)**.

CIAC first opened to display modern art in 1998 when the moving spirits behind the good idea were expatriate Irish artists

Empyrius 1999 Anne Madden   53 sqm   Oil on canvas   The International Centre of Contemporary Art, Château de Carros

Anne Madden (*b*. 1932) and her husband, Louis le Brocquy (1916–2012), who lived nearby at Domaine Le Combes for many years. Anne Madden was invited by the mayor to paint a small vaulted ceiling of a room on the first floor with two diminutive windows, one looking out onto the landscape and the other to the sea. She covered the semi-circular ceiling with brilliant organic brushstrokes of cobalt blue, on which she superimposed a glowing golden inner circle of loose brushstrokes, to realise a breathtaking, poetic new work of abstract art which she titled *Empyrius*. It is a true masterpiece. She generously donated the installation to CIAC, and it was inaugurated in 1999. It is on permanent view in summer when the building is open to the public, and it is a most beautiful and imaginative interpretation of a poetic theme in a challenging and difficult space. Art critic Marcelin Pleynet has described it as a tour de force, which it is. The artist herself said she drew her inspiration from the blues of the sea and the sky, and the golden light of the Mediterranean sun.

CIAC underwent a second period of refurbishment and re-opened to the public in 2010 revealing fine marble staircases, banisters and smooth cream-coloured walls which are ideal for displaying modern art. Salle Anne Madden et Louis le Brocquy is one of the best exhibition spaces on the second floor.

The centre now concentrates on two or three comprehensive exhibitions by living artists in the Riviera region each year. In 2014 it featured the paintings, painted sculptures, drawings and books by artist Jean-Jacques Laurent (*b*. 1943). Laurent works in a brutalist figurative style reminiscent of Dubuffet and even Louis Cane from Beaulieu, and taking inspiration from ancient prehistoric cave paintings – though it must be said that Laurent is a very individualistic artist.

The centre has also accumulated a permanent collection of paintings, sculptures and graphics over the years, by some 130 artists who worked throughout the Riviera region, and these are exhibited occasionally. It includes work by Appel, Arman, César, Gaudet, Kijno, Isnard, Klein, Léger, Miguel, Picasso, Ubac, Villers and others.

Lemon in the Hand 1973   **Louis Le Brocquy** HRHA (1916–2012) Oil on canvas

Some interesting relics of the ancient château have been preserved in the refurbishment of the building, and they add to the experience of visiting. Outside of the entrance stands a ten-pointed wood and plexiglass abstract sculpture that should have twelve upright sentinels, but two have gone missing over the years. No artist's name is attached, and there is no sign to state that it is under repair.

The tiny village of **Le Broc**, a further four kilometres on from Carros Village, is worth visiting simply for the panoramic views over the mountains and the valley of the Var, and for the **Ancient Baroque Chapel** which contains an important religious painting by Jean Canavesio of the sixteenth century. It also has a restaurant that serves a wholesome lunch.

After Cannes on the return journey to Nice, near the bridge over the Var, visitors should look out for *La Barque*, a splendid large abstract steel multi-tined sculpture painted brown and cream, by the eminent contemporary Côte d'Azur artist Bernard Pagès (*b.* 1940). It is a particularly fine example of that major artist's inimitable style, which is instantly recognisable even from a fleeting glance from a bus. You can't stop immediately to admire it, as it is aptly sited on a roundabout on that busy motorway.

Turn off the grey in your life and light the colours inside you.

Pablo Picasso

Grasse is one of France's leading perfume producers. The very air of Grasse is delicately perfumed by the hundreds of thousands of fragrant roses, lavender, jasmine and orange blossom that bloom in abundance all about the region to supply the production of exotic perfumes. It is the home town of Fragonard, Negre, Mallet and Gérard and if you are interested in old masters and artefacts from as far back as prehistory, a day spent in Grasse will be well-rewarded. It has at least four small interesting museums and a stunning ancient cathedral. If you are only interested in modern art, give Grasse a miss.

The **Cathedral Notre-Dame-du-Puy** is a great sombre stone Romanesque building dating from as early as the twelfth century. Massive round pillars support a high narrow nave vaulted with heavy ogives and side balconies that look primitive and unchanged since the Middle Ages. But the Cathedral is softened and enhanced by fine paintings, impressive stone sculptures, and early religious artefacts of fine quality. Let us start with the three strong paintings by the great Flemish artist Peter Paul Rubens (1577–1640), painted by him at the early age of twenty-four. They have been hanging in the cathedral since 1827, when they were bequeathed by a M. Perolle. All three are of equal large size, with rounded tops, and must have originally been painted for specific spaces, perhaps in Flanders. They hang side by side on the right side of the cathedral. The first painting *Crucifixion of Christ*, 1602, depicts the crucified Christ surrounded by attendants. It is a fine composition and is powerfully painted. The second is a vision of

The number 500 bus from Nice takes you through some lovely winding country roads to the ancient town of Grasse, famous for its perfumes. It takes about an hour and a quarter to get there, and a bus timetable is a useful thing to have in your pocket to time your return journey, since buses are not very frequent on the route.

Jeune fille délivrant un oiseau de sa cage 1775 Jean-Honoré Fragonard Oil on canvas

Saint Hélène in exaltation by the cross. The saint wears a handsome brown robe with an intricate pattern, and again the composition is strong and the brushwork colourful and free. The third painting, also dated 1602, is *The Crowning with Thorns*, and here the artist brilliantly captures the agony of Christ surrounded by his torturers. The paintings make a glorious trio. Rubens left Antwerp to visit Rome in 1601, where he studied the works of earlier masters Raphael and Caravaggio, and I speculate that these three works were painted in Rome under their influence.

The Holy Sacrament Chapel is a large area that extends to the right of the cathedral nave and is a most impressive space. Larger-than-life statues of Saints Mark, Matthew, Luke and John look out from above eye-level niches, two on each side. On the back wall hangs a large oil painting on canvas by the local eighteenth-century master Jean-Honoré Fragonard. It is *The Washing of Feet* and portrays Christ humbly kneeling and washing the feet of poor people. It is beautifully painted in bright colours, the humility and pathos of the scene perfectly captured by Fragonard in what must be a rare religious painting by him. Over the altar is a moving portrait by the outstanding Niçois artist Ludovico Brea of Saint-Honorat who was born in Arles in the fifth century. Saint-Honorat with his followers founded the abbey on one of the islands of Lérins. This island is now named Saint-Honorat. The people of Nice named a side street, rue Brea, after their famous painter family.

On the other side of the nave is a powerful big painting, *Death of Saint Paul,* 1848, by Grasse artist Charles Negre. It stands out for the honesty and skill with which the artist has interpreted the scene, and is a fine realistic work of the Victorian period. A few other paintings hang in less important spaces, said to be by Subleyras and Gaillard. These are accompanied by exceptional examples of fifteenth-century polychrome figures of religious significance. A massive organ fills the cathedral with sonorous music on Sundays during the celebration of mass, which still attracts a good mustering of the older inhabitants.

Grasse became the episcopal see of the Catholic Church in France in 1244. The nearby bishop's palace is now the **Hôtel de Ville**. A fountain in the front courtyard has a relief carved sculpture of a beautiful seated young woman by local sculptor Rabuis, and she is said to symbolise the extensive presence of perfume manufacturing in the region. On the corner of place du Petit Puy is a tall stone tower, Tour du Guet, still in excellent repair. A plaque commemorates the Grassois poet and man of letters of the sixteenth century, Antoine Godeau (1603–72), who was a member of the Académie Française.

In the middle of the old town is the **Oratory Chapel** built in 1632. Mass is still celebrated there, though part of this Franciscan church seems to have been subsumed into a perfumery and a department store.

The **Fragonard Museum** is on rue Jean Ossola in the old town and is housed in a beautifully refurbished historic town house. The museum is dedicated to the town's most celebrated citizen, the painter J. H. Fragonard (1732–1806), and to two lesser-known Grasse artists of the following generation, Jean-Baptiste Mallet (1759–1835) and Marguerite Gérard (1761–1832), who was Fragonard's sister-in-law. Local perfumier Jean-François Costa (1921–2012) of the Fragonard Perfume Factory started collecting the paintings of these local artists in the 1950s and recently donated them to the museum, which is sponsored by the Fragonard Perfumery. Fragonard studied under French masters Boucher and Chardin and painted scantily clad young women in frivolous, amusing situations, but with great skill and a wonderful colour sense.

Fragonard's paintings are scattered about in museums throughout the world, so Mr Costa did well to accumulate enough to grace a room in the museum. Of particular note is *Jeune fille délivrant un oiseau de sa cage*, an oil dated 1770–75. It is said to be a portrait of a famous actress, and an allegory of chastity. The young woman is holding onto the bird with a slight ribbon and keeping it from escape, just as she must preserve her virginity until she marries, which is by no means easy. Fragonard did adore the many beautiful, voluptuous young women who surrounded him, and he made every excuse to portray them in various guises and revealing states of dress and undress. A second room contains a number of Fragonard's drawings in pencil and sanguine. He could draw in a masterly fashion, as these reveal. The room also contains a set of tighter, small pencil drawings of Fragonard and his family; these are said to be by him, but I doubt it. They were found in an attic and are very different in style from the signed, authenticated, fluent pencil and wash drawings that hang near them. One of these tighter sketches is of a dog with the head of a man and dated *c.* 1788. It is competent and amusing.

The room with Marguerite Gérard's paintings reveals an artist with genuine individual style and talent who was previously unknown to me. Her painting *Young Mother Bathing Her Child*, dated 1800–10, is fresh and most competent. I adjudge her a better artist than J. B. Mallet, who occupies the third room and whose stiffer style was based on the study of Dutch painters.

The basement of the museum shows videos of artists, and in 2014 held an exhibition of exotic travel photographs by the Russian Sergei Prokudin-Gorski (1843–1944). Curiously, the shop upstairs sells perfumes and souvenirs of Grasse but contains no postcard reproductions of the paintings in the museum collection. What a pity! The emphasis is on the Fragonard Perfumery but this can be excused, I suppose, because Mr Costa's generosity has made the whole thing possible.

The building in which the works of art are housed was apparently once the Hôtel de Villeneuve, built in the seventeenth century by the eminent Provençal family, the cultivated Villeneuves, who were descended from Romée le Grand, the Baron of Vence from 1231 to 1250. Interestingly, it was also the home of the Comte

d'Artagnan, the King's musketeer and cousin to the celebrated d'Artagnan of Alexandre Dumas's novels. It was purchased by Mr Costa and now belongs to the Fragonard Perfumery.

The **Musée d'Art et d'Histoire de Provence (MAHP)** on rue Mirabeau, Grasse, is open daily and is a fascinating surprise. Entry is free and there are lots of fine artefacts from the past to see. There is very good furniture and many portraits of eminent ladies and gentlemen, most of whom were painted by artists long forgotten and not recorded. An exception is a very good full-length portrait by Charles Negre in the nineteenth century, of a former owner of the house, Général Comte Gazan de la Peyrière, in full military uniform. Another is a group portrait in oils of the Isnard family by Francesco Pascucci in 1804.

Downstairs there is an extensive collection of faience tableware of the seventeenth and eighteenth centuries from the best manufacturing areas of France at that time. There is also a room full of antique children's toys, including a doll's house complete with miniature furnishings.

The most fascinating room is one that contains endless ceramic bowls and implements from prehistoric to Greek and Roman times in the province. There are ceramic oil lamps, and even a Roman skeleton lying full-length in a long glass case. There are also two rather fine polychromed religious carvings from the Middle Ages, one of them riddled with, presumably dead, woodworms.

Another room contains an olive press and a dozen massive ceramic jars in which the oil was stored. The basement rooms lead out into a most elegant garden which is well-tended and ideal for adults with children. Finally, two little unframed oil paintings by the much-mentioned Charles Negre show that there was more to him than portraiture and religious art.

These are delicious little studies of reclining naked ladies, one of whom, Leda, is about to be ravished by a male swan. It ended my enjoyable visit to a museum that gives more than it promises.

The **Musée Parfumerie Fragonard** is located in a house which dates from 1782 but only became the perfume museum in 1926. Don't miss it. It has a collection of items such as jewellery and precious perfume bottles covering 3,000 years of the history of perfume, from antique Egyptian, Greek and Roman items to the present date. It is also graced by period paintings of flowers and portraits, and comes up to date with modern portraits of the Costa family. Outside the museum is a small bronze public sculpture titled *Habit de Parfumeur* of 1997, by Polish artist Tomek Kawiak (*b.* 1943) after a seventeenth-century engraving. It features a little girl of yesteryear laden down with bottles of perfume and bags of fragrant herbs for sale. It is a sentimental work but very charming and much photographed by tourists.

The most prominent sculpture in the town centre is that of the celebrated J. H. Fragonard, portrayed in white with palette in hand and accompanied by a cherub with a beautiful woman leaning over him. Fashioned by Auguste Maillard (1864–1944) in 1907, it is a fitting tribute to the famous local son.

There are a few more modern sculptures dotted about the town telling us that Grasse holds an International Sculpture Conference at regular intervals. These include an attractive white marble flower form sited at the bus terminal, by Iranian artist Majid Haghigbi from the 4th Symposium in 2012, and the appealing *Pétale* by Ruth Geber from Hungary from the 1st Symposium in 2005.

If I don't have red I use blue. Pablo Picasso

A new spirit of art is about in Monaco these days, with the emphasis on contemporary art and not the old masters. The tiny independent principality of approximately 2 sq km is one of the most densely populated areas of the world, many of its inhabitants are extremely rich and enjoy a very favourable tax regime. Monaco is not part of France, but it is part of the French Riviera and has good views of the Italian Riviera over the nearby French border. It is home to the princely Rainiers who held sway over much of the French Riviera for many centuries in the past.

The number 100 bus from MAMAC at Garibaldi in Nice gets you to Monaco in forty-five minutes, and the coastal views are incomparable along the way. Perhaps the best place to start looking at modern art is to take a number 2 municipality bus from Port Hercule. It winds its way up the steep hill to eventually stop at the Jardin Exotique near the recently refurbished white Villa Paloma, which opened to the public in 2014 with important exhibitions by leading international artists. The lovely building, set in a magnificent Italian-style garden, was only built in 1913 and was acquired by the State in 1995. It was given to the **Nouveau Musée National de Monaco (NMNM)** in 2008 and inaugurated as an exhibition wing of the museum towards the end of 2010. The museum is now situated in two locations, the **Villa Sauber** and the **Villa Paloma**. In spring 2014 it put on a comprehensive retrospective exhibition of over 135 works by the renowned Swiss-American sculptor-painter Richard Artschwager (1923–2013), who won a major award at the Venice Biennale in his lifetime.

From June to early November 2014 NMNM featured a unique selection of pictures by the Gilbert and George duo of artists from London who have lived together since their first meeting at St Martin's School of Art in 1967. The two young men, one Italian and the other English, have worked together as one single and fiercely independent artist since then, achieving world renown for their controversial performance sculptures and photo-based multi-panel pictures that challenge all conventions and ignore all criticism. The works were elegantly displayed over the three floors of the lovely villa, which retains two most attractive stained-glass windows on the theme of birds and flowers by the master glazier of Nice, Fassi Cadet, installed in 1950 after war damage. The exhibition was accompanied by a thoughtful explanatory booklet by critic Michael Bracewell, and by a full-length film on the two-in-one artists which gives us a fascinating insight into how they think, work and live near Brick Lane in east London.

On the way out of the museum there is an admirable painted epoxy resin sculpture titled *Cloche-Poche*, 1973–88, by the French artist Jean Dubuffet (1901–85); it is a striking feature of the well-tended garden.

The admission fee to the Villa Paloma is €6, but you may purchase a multiple ticket for €10 which entitles you to visit the larger **Exotic Garden** nearby with its extraordinary collection of rare plants, as well as the **Musée d'Anthropologie Préhistorique** and the beautiful Villa Sauber downtown near Monte Carlo. The historic museum is of limited interest. It is small and contains skulls, bones and recreations of woolly mammoths, giant deer and bison which once inhabited the Riviera coastal region. It also displays Iron Age weapons and modern paintings of hunting scenes of mediocre quality. The museum was founded by Prince Albert I in 1902 and inaugurated in its new premises in 1959 by Prince Rainier III, who married the glamourous Irish-American film star Grace Kelly.

The next destination is Villa Sauber at Larvotto, the sister museum of Villa Paloma run by NMNM. It was owned by English painter Robert Sauber from 1904, and is reputed to have been designed by Charles Garnier, who built the Paris Opera House around the same time. This beautiful belle époque villa is one of the loveliest in Monaco. It has been handsomely refurbished to display contemporary art, including innovative video screenings titled *Portraits d'Intérieurs* in an exhibition in summer 2014. On the way in to the villa is an impressive white marble Venus, *c.*1911, by Léopold Bernstamm, tempting visitors from her grotto. She is brazenly sculpted from white Carrara marble by the relatively unknown artist from Riga, who captured her magnificent contours with exquisite mastery and passion. The interiors exhibition was very avant-garde and thought-provoking.

The artists participating included Marc-Camille Chaimowicz, Danika Dakic, Brice Dellsperger, Nick Mauss and Laura Prouvoust, who in some instances made new installations, sometimes using small works by other artists to illustrate their concepts. Of particular note was Nick Mauss's installation painting using cotton appliqué on velvet with painted brass door knobs and a doorstopper. The mustard, black and white overall transformation of the space stops you in your tracks. Chaimowicz's installation tribute to Jean Cocteau was also a moving experience: an imagined room filled with borrowed and created objects, including a plaster and polychrome relief sculpture of 1958 by Cocteau himself titled *Le Grand Dieu Pan*, which is now in the permanent collection of NMNM.

The next space to visit is the most important one in the municipality for lovers of modern art: the massive, recently built **Grimaldi Forum** nearby. It is the venue of choice in the region for annual blockbuster art exhibitions. In 2013 it featured what was claimed to be the largest exhibition of paintings and drawings by Picasso ever held. They all came from the private Syrian collector Nahmad, who normally stores them in his private museum near Geneva airport. The huge exhibition was mind-boggling. Picasso in old age did not always paint masterpieces. The Picasso Museum in Paris demonstrates this also. But when he was brilliant he was truly incomparable, and the exhibition of 2013 proved this. The only periods under-represented were Picasso's early cubist and blue periods.

In 2014 the Grimaldi Forum had another blockbuster exhibition, from the private collection of M. Pinault, chairman of Christie's auction house. It was a stunning exhibition of large works by big-name international contemporaries. Pride of place was given to *Hanging Heart*, 1994–2006, made from mirror-polished stainless steel with transparent colour coating by the American artist Jeff Koons, (*b.* 1955). Koons's sculptures sell for millions of dollars each year, and he employs at least eighty-four personal assistants in his factory studio in New York. Some art connoisseurs consider Koons a charlatan who creates banal images, but only time will tell. Fellow-American sculptor Paul McCarthy, (*b.* 1945), was represented by a massive stainless steel female torso complete with see-through holes, wittily titled

Henry Moore Bound to Fail Maquette. British sculptor Rachel Whiteread, (*b.* 1963), filled a whole room with her *Untitled* (a hundred cast resin spaces in subtle varying colours). Fellow British *enfant terrible* Damien Hirst, (*b.* 1965), showed paintings in the manner of Francis Bacon and a four-part sculpture of cows' heads in formaldehyde cubes, titled *Matthew, Mark, Luke and John.* The famous Japanese lens-based artist, Hiroshi Sugimoto, (*b.* 1948), showed an arresting, elongated modern take on *The Last Supper* by Leonardo da Vinci. Deceased American artist Dan Flavin (1933–96) was represented by a characteristic neon light piece in red and yellow, titled *Alternative Diagonals* of 1964, as a tribute to his artist friend, the celebrated minimalist sculptor Donald Judd (1928–94).

A special feature of this Grimaldi Forum exhibition was that viewers were invited to pick up an illustrated explanatory sheet of related works of art located elsewhere with a particular bearing on the works on show. The whole show was exhilarating, as was the Picasso show the previous year. The Forum is not to be missed. Its sponsors obviously have considerable resources to support contemporary art, and M. Pinault is one of the mainstays of the international contemporary art market. The Forum is also used for conferences and trade exhibitions when not in use as a temporary art museum.

After the Forum it is hard to look at any older art. A walk through the **Princess Grace Japanese Garden** is a suitable relaxant for a jaded viewer. Along the route leading to the **Palais Princier** perched on a high outcrop of rock (Le Rocher) are some spectacular architectural buildings, such as the famous ornate **Casino de Monte Carlo** of 1863 by Garnier, the magnificent **Hôtel de Paris** nearby, and the tiny eleventh-century chapel dedicated to Monaco's patron saint, Sainte-Dévote. This is sandwiched between colossal modern high-rise buildings which could almost be described as skyscrapers. There are other churches worth visiting on another day, including the **Chapel of Mercy**, built in 1939 on rue Basse, and the baroque **Musée de la Chapelle de la Visitation**, which contains religious scenes by Ribera and Rubens, thanks to a private donor. One passes bronze sculptures of Formula I racing cars, reminding us that this is a traditional sport for which Monte Carlo is famous. Prince Rainier III had his very own museum of vintage cars, and there are a number of other museums in the principality for eager beavers.

The changing of the guard at the Palais du Prince is enjoyable, but the paintings in the palace are of lesser quality than the sumptuous furnishings and objets d'art which adorn the ornate interior.

Monaco offers an eclectic sculpture trail to be followed by fit devotees, who will discover more than a hundred works in public places if they persevere. It is impressive, and one could spend an entire day viewing the works of local and international artists dotted about the principality in prominent positions. They are mainly concentrated in the **Fontvieille District**, and that is a good place to start. There are so many works of interest that it is almost unfair to pick some out. But among the standouts are Fernando Botero's witty *Woman Smoking a Cigarette* and Lynn Chadwick's typical angular *Sitting Couple*, the male with a rectangular head and the female with a triangular one. In the **UNESCO Garden** the mosaic *Three Musicians* by Fernand Léger is noteworthy. The Italian artist, Arnoldo Pomodoro (*b.* 1926), is represented by a cast of his beautiful polished *Sphere Within Sphere*, another cast of which stands on a plinth in front of the new reading room in Trinity College, Dublin. Renoir, assisted by Richard Guino, created the wonderful *Large Washerwoman*, cast in bronze and appropriately sited in a fountain.

The Colombian artist Fernando Botero (*b.* 1932) has a second work, *Adam and Eve*, two massive bronze figures in the Monte Carlo area. The bronze, neo-academic *Il Cardinal Seduto* (Seated Cardinal) of 1982 by Italian sculptor Giacomo Manzú (1908–1991) is appropriately sited on a plinth on the forecourt of the **Church of Saint-Charles**, where it is highly visible to bus passengers returning from Menton.
The most famous name in the collection and in my opinion the best sculptor of the twentieth century is British sculptor Henry Moore (1898–1986). His bronze in the collection is titled *Three Part Object*, and is vaguely suggestive of a female form, though the elements are abstracted and transformed. It stands on a stone plinth on the terrace

of the **Princess Grace Theatre**. There are many works by Arman, including a typical bronze composition of sliced cellos in an upright stack that is instantly recognisable. Less obvious and a nice surprise is the figurative knight with spear comforting a maiden, titled *Ettore and Andromaca*, by the Italian artist Giorgio de Chirico, who is better known for his metaphysical paintings. It is sited in the **Saint-Martin Gardens**. Concluding this snapshot is the brown patinated figure of Malizia at the entrance to the **Grimaldi Palace** on the hill, which will need an extended visit to fully experience the treasures contained within. The sculpture is by Kees Verkade but its special significance is that it is a representation of a Grimaldi forebear, François Grimaldi, who centuries ago dressed up as a Franciscan monk to gain entrance to the fortress and capture it with the help of his followers.

The Grimaldis have inhabited Monaco since 1297 when it was captured by Francesco Grimaldi cunningly disguised as a monk. They only became princes of the town in 1604, and the title continues to the present time. The château they inhabit looks comparatively new, but that is not the case, and you should pay the entrance fee to appreciate the magnificence of the interior frescoed sixteenth-century courtyard. It is called the **Galerie d'Hercule** and occupies the site of the original ancient château, which was a fortified fort with cannon guns on the ramparts to ward off pirates on the rampage.

A monumental white Carrara staircase leads up to the castle entrance. The castle contains much fine French period furniture and historic family portraits, but lacks great masterpieces. Any that once hung there were probably plundered during the French Revolution to pay taxes as was the case with the splendid portrait of Marchesa Maria Grimaldi with dwarf, (*c.*1607) by Rubens. It is now in the Kingston Lacy Estate of the U.K. National Trust.

A notable portrait still hangs there of the famed art collector Cardinal Mazarin by Nicolas Mignard (1606–68). Near the entrance is a portrait of the late Princess Grace (née Patricia Grace Kelly) by Ricardo Macarron of 1974. In it she is seated wearing a red gown against the background of sea-green/blue. It seems a better work of art than the 1956 portrait of her by Ralph Wolfe Cowan. This latter artist also painted a family group portrait of the Rainiers in 2005, and it is a truly awful, banal painting though it records for posterity the prince and princess with their son Albert and daughters Caroline and Stephanie, before the princess died in a tragic car crash. What a pity they were not better advised in choosing the painter of their portraits. The early twentieth-century portrait of an ancestor, Prince Louis of Monaco, by the Hungarian Philip de László (1869–1937), is much more stylish and accomplished.

You can avail of an audio guide to inform you of the contents and history of each ornate room on the visitor route. There is an armoury with an impressive display of guns. **The Pompeian Salon** has French ornate period furniture which once belonged to the artist aristocrat Henri de Toulouse Lautrec (1864–1901). The Gallery of Mirrors displays bronze busts of Prince and Princess Rainier and wedding presents sent from Egypt and China. **The Duke of York Salon** is so named because an English Duke died in that room on his travels. The **Red Room** contains a seventeenth-century painting of the *Head of Christ* in the manner of the Italian master Guido Reni (1575–1642). The **Yellow Salon** is particularly elegant. It contains exquisite Boule tables and a rare eighteenth-century Moustiers plate bearing the Grimaldi coat of arms. The ancestor portraits are impressive here. Princess Louise-Hippolyte was painted by J. B. Van Loo (1684–1745), Jacques de Matignon by Nicolas Largillière (1656–1746), and there are two others by Hyacinthe Rigaud (1659–1743). The Blue Room has yet more portraits and scenes of historic interest. The **Louis XIII Bedroom** has paintings attributed to well-known names. The finest picture is titled *The Music Lesson* and is attributed to Titian. The Throne Room has, of course, the official throne on which the prince sits on formal occasions when he is receiving guests. It also has many portraits on the walls, but a distinguishing feature is the fine stone fireplace and chimney, constructed from La Turbie Quarry. As visitors and guests leave they pass through the **Anti-Chamber Matignon** where there is a model of a yacht named *La Minerva* on display, presented to the family by the Greek shipping magnate, Aristotle Onassis.

Wisely, the private family quarters are not on public view. An excellent illustrated guidebook tells us that they enjoy a private garden with swimming pool, and go to church in the baroque Chapelle Saint-Jean-Baptiste, which contains fresco scenes from the life of Sainte-Dévote, the patron saint of the principality, painted by German artists. The saint is further venerated in a stained-glass panel by Chartres master Nicolas Losin. The bedrooms contain tapestries and objets d'art including ornate ceramics.

It is a real pleasure to visit the seat of the Grimaldis and stroll down afterwards to the cathedral where Princess Grace and Prince Rainier are buried. It is well worth a visit before you proceed to lunch or dinner at one of the many restaurants on the hilltop. The view of the harbour as you descend by the steps to sea level is memorable and picturesque. It is just the place to delay and take a souvenir photograph or two.

Monaco also has very many commercial galleries, too many to mention individually, which sell expensive works of art. Some years ago one leading gallery in Monte Carlo had as many as nine Picasso oil paintings on view in the window for sale. Another prominent commercial gallery in the Monte Carlo vicinity specialises in the sale of Russian Masters. One can only speculate on the number and quality of fine art that must exist there in private residences, unknown to the general public.

Modern architecture in Monaco

The most pleasant way to visit the attractive, ancient town of Mouans-Sartoux is by train. A day return ticket from Nice Gare Centrale costs €13.20 and gets you there in an hour or thereabouts. Alternatively, if you are driving, it is just north of Mougins and you take the N85 towards Grasse.

Like many other towns and villages in the region, Mouans-Sartoux has an ancient history. In 1592 the Duke of Savoy punished the inhabitants of the village for their allegiance to Henry III and burnt the Château de Mouans-Sartoux to the ground in the sixteenth century. Its owner, the widowed Suzanne de Villeneuve, clearly a woman of determination, pursued the Duke through the Cagnes plains and forced payment from him. The château was rebuilt and is a most handsome triangular edifice with a bastion or tower at each corner. It became the property of the citizens of the town in 1989 and an impressive exhibition space was created. **Espace de l'Art Concret** was inaugurated in 1990 as a permanent centre for contemporary art.

The inspiration for this change of function came from the Swiss abstract artist Gottfried Honegger (1917–2016) and his astute wife the art collector Sybil Albers-Barrier. They donated their private art collection by important modern abstract artists to the town on the understanding that a suitable new building would be erected in the grounds of the château to house the collection. That came to pass in 2004 with an abstract minimal new eco-friendly museum near the trees of the chateau, designed and built by architects Gigon/Guyer of Zurich and suitably painted pale green. It blends discreetly into the background of the château gardens. In 2003 they also built an unusual small outdoor exhibition space in the woods for the display of children's art, known as **Préau des Enfants**, after French architect Marc Barani designed and built the Atelier Pédagogique at the back of the château in 1998 for pedagogical activities for children and young people. The Préau des Enfants, deep within the wood, has open sides and is an imaginative, open-sided space. You could be forgiven for thinking the collection you were travelling to see might be works

of sculpture made from concrete. Not at all! Rather, the description for that rigorously abstract type of art was first formulated in Paris in 1930 by a dedicated group of artists led by Theo Van Doesburg and including Jean Hélion, Marcel Wantz and Otto Gustav Carlsund. They published their manifesto which called for modern artists to make use of the circle, the square and the rectangle and variations thereof, combined with pure colours, to create a new non-representational art that was the antithesis of impressionism. They believed in mechanical, exact techniques that ignored nature but expressed its spirituality, and they succeeded in producing a startling body of new art, as this collection beautifully illustrates. The year 2014 celebrated ten years of the new museum's existence by presenting choice selections from the overall donation by the following artists: Bernard Aubertin, Max Bill, Sonia Delaunay-Terk, herman de vries, Gottfried Honegger, John McCracken, François Morellet, Francois Perrodin, Aurélie Nemours, Adrian Schiess, Alan Charlton and Bernar Venet. It was a most impressive selection and presentation of minimal, imaginative modern abstract art. Each artist had his or her own space, and the overall effect was calming and uplifting.

Hommage à Ken Saro-Wiwa 1996 Gottfried Honegger Silkscreen

The overall standard was very high, but of particular appeal were the geometric paintings of Swiss artist and architect Max Bill (1908–94) and the French sculptor François Morellet's *Sphere-trams*, 1970 – a steel-mesh ball suspended on a thin wire from the ceiling. Dutch artist de Vries from Alkmaar showed pictures composed with dead brown leaves, beautifully mounted and arranged on paper and protected by glass. Honegger himself is revealed as a very fine artist. He was born in Switzerland in 1917 and lived in Zurich with his wife Sybil, when they were not residing in Mouans-Sartoux. In 2014, at the age ninety-seven years, he returned to Mouans-Sartoux for the official opening of the Ten Years Exhibition. He died in January 2016. His diptych *Tableau-Relief R 1237* of 1997 in shades of black and grey was a thing of rare beauty. The museum always displays the permanent collection in the new museum building.

The admission cost of €7 allows the visitor access to both the new museum and the château, which contains equally entrancing alternative exhibitions of other artists. The château has an exciting programme annually of presenting high-quality temporary exhibitions on selected themes such as the body, geometric abstraction, etc. Both buildings have small shops selling postcards, books, and in the case of the château, original lithographs and limited-edition facsimiles by the artists in the donation. A press pack is available for visitors.

Honegger porcelain plates sell for €150 each, and the château contained a serigraph by him, titled *Untitled (Blue)*, and numbered 23 from an edition of 24, available for €660 framed. It was a delightful minimal study of a blue square with black lines on a white ground, where the colours sing and positioning of the geometric forms is just perfect. It would make a lovely gift or souvenir for oneself or another. At the entrance to the château is a handsome upright geometric marble sculpture with peep slot by German artist Ulrich Ruckriem (*b.* 1938) and a further flat granite square set into the ground by the same artist.

The château has been beautifully transformed into an all-white exhibition space, with many separate rooms which are ideal for contemporary art. An exhibited poster featured Serbian performance artist Marina Abramović (*b.* 1946) with her former partner Ulay performing *Rest Energy*, 1980, which was premiered at the Rosc International art Exhibition in Dublin that year. On that occasion she stood still for four minutes and ten seconds while her partner aimed a deadly arrow at her exposed breast from a fully drawn longbow, and neither of them moved a fraction of an inch for the entire performance. Abramović was wearing a simple white shirt and dress. The audience was fully aware that the slightest mistake on Ulay's part, through tiredness or inattention, could result in Abramović's immediate death. She was and still is a daring, imaginative risk-taker. A second work by her in the château exhibition was a video titled *Stromboli (Head)*, which showed the artist's head lying on the shore of a sea that constantly washed against her face, and possibly over it.

Ligne horizontale passant sur trois carrés 1974 François Morellet Acrylic on canvas

She lay there wet and unflinching for an undefined period of time. Also appealing were the nine acrylic paintings on paper in soft shades of green and yellow, forming a single work of art by Marthe Wéry (1930–2005) from a private collection. Perhaps the most intriguing work in the exhibition was by Sino-British artist Su-Mei Tse, titled *Bird Cage*, 2007. It is constructed from tube neon light, and the large glowing cage with open door is mounted on a Chinese black lacquer stand. It too is from a private collection. This second exhibition in the château was titled *À Corps Perdu* and contained works by other well-known artists, including Roni Horn, Roman Opalka, Thomas Vinson, and Jürgen Klauke.

Elsewhere in the **Château Gardens** you will come across good examples of sculpture by Bernar Venet and Gottfried Honegger. The latter donated a particularly large blue painted metal sculpture dated 1997 to the town of Mouans-Sartoux, and it stands in a place of honour in his memory on a roundabout at the entrance to the town.

The former stables of the château beside the entrance gate are now a small, informative museum of rural life as lived in bygone days. In 2014 it was freshened up extensively by a local contractor in concert with ongoing maintenance of the internal fabric of the château.

In the charming old town centre there is the small plain church of **St-André,** outside the gates of the château. It is worth a visit to see the simple but lovely eight modern abstract stained-glass windows designed, by Honegger, which contrast so interestingly with five older representational windows. The church exudes a feeling of calm and contemplation, enhanced by the view of a large wood carving of *Christ on the Cross* over the little altar stone. The relatively new church was built on the site of the 1496 Priory of St-André.

The major French sculptor Bernar Venet, who lives outside Draguignan at Le Muy, has set up his own personal Foundation there and it is open to the public. Mouans-Sartoux is a most delightful surprise, and I recommend it highly to visitors to the Riviera.

Some of the best preserved belle époque architecture along the coast is in the charming seaside town of Beaulieu-sur-Mer or Beaulieu. This includes the beautiful **Villa Grecque Kérylos** which is a short walk down a narrow road from the centre of Beaulieu. Guiding you on your way is a bronze bust of Greek statesman Eleftherios Venizelos on a plinth at the corner of the narrow road. As you walk past a large gated mansion, a notice informs you it was once the residence of the famous architect and engineer Gustave Eiffel, who built many amazing structures throughout France, including the famous Eiffel tower in Paris. The Villa Kérylos is just around the corner on a promontory looking down onto the Bristol Marina, with its many boats and small yachts corralled in the corner, and out over the blue bay of the Port des Fourmis, which translates as port of ants. If you look across the bay you will have a spectacular view of Cap Ferrat.

Cap Ferrat, with the Port of Saint Jean in the middle, has the massive pink and white edifice of Villa Ephrussi de Rothschild, surrounded by its many gardens, on top of the hill near the cape's narrowest part. The area is now home to the rich and famous in their private villas and their yachts and boats.

The Villa Kérylos was built during the period 1902–1908 by Théodore Reinach, the third son of a rich German businessman of Jewish extraction who moved to Paris in the nineteenth century and made an even greater fortune there through his astute business acumen. Curiously, the three Reinach sons never attended State schools but

The number 98 bus from beside MAMAC and Place Yves Klein in Nice will take you fairly quickly to both Beaulieu-sur-Mer and Cap Ferrat, where two major cultural venues are worth visiting. If you are energetic and prepared to walk between the two venues, I suggest starting early. and purchasing a combined ticket for €20 which admits you to both villas. Alternatively, you may prefer to take two days to explore this beautiful terrain, as there are other sights worth experiencing on the Cap peninsula. Both villas open at 10 am in summer.

instead had their own private tutor. They were also taught to take a wide interest in culture and business affairs by their ambitious father. They grew up mixing with bankers, politicians and artists, and each displayed exceptional intelligence and enthusiasm for life. Théodore, the youngest, became an expert on archaic Greek art and wrote on the subject. One of the other brothers became a museum director. All three acquired the reputation of being 'know-it-alls'. Théodore's passion for Greek culture became such an obsession that when he visited wealthy Beaulieu on vacation at the beginning of the twentieth century, it so reminded him of Greece that he decided to build a Greek villa there in which to live and to entertain distinguished guests. At first he did not move in local high society in Beaulieu, but this did not deter him from eventually inviting kings and princes to this fascinating reproduction of a fifth-century villa of a wealthy, aristocratic citizen of Athens. It was elegantly crammed with precious ceramics, bronzes and coins which he had collected in his archaeological pursuits. His first wife died young, and he remarried a niece of Béatrice Ephrussi de Rothschild whose mansion he could see across the bay from the windows of his villa. His children and grandchildren remained living in the villa after his death until 1967, when it was handed over to the State and designated a historic building.

Inside the entrance door is a sunken mosaic and marble bathroom with both hot and cold water, in the ancient style which it copies. In the Peristyle or main courtyard which follows on from there, Reinach used to entertain his many invited guests, who included Gustave Eiffel, the dancer Isadora Duncan and the actress Sarah Bernhardt, as well as visiting royalty. The walls here are frescoed in the manner of French painter Pierre-Puvis de Chavannes (1824–98), and the themes are of the twelve main Greek gods with their human attributes of goodness and badness. One fresco portrays Athenians about to sacrifice a bull to appease the gods on Mount Olympus. There is an impressive library, well stocked with bound books, and fine examples of pre-Christian decorated Greek pots as well as bronzes and large amphorae recovered from the sea. Nearby is a bronze replica of a statue of the goddess Athena by the great fifth-century BC sculptor Phidias. Beside it is an even more rare sculpture, a bronze original of Auriga of Delphos, a charioteer dressed in a furrowed robe dating from the fifth-century BC and described as an example of Severe Art, a style of early classical sculpture. Among the more striking small items are a bronze head of a young man with open see-through eye slits, and a menacing Greek war helmet in a display case with many oil lamps and other ceramic objects.

A curiosity is the lemonwood folding piano made especially for the villa by Pleyel in the twentieth century. Such pianos were used sometimes in re-enactments of ancient Greek songs and dances. Near it is a large metal copy of a *cratere* or *krater* in which wine and water were mixed in Greek ceremonies. Reinach's bedroom, which he called the Eros room, has wonderful views from its windows. The floor is a fine mosaic design copied from ancient discoveries. His bed is a faithful reproduction of a rich man's bed in Plato's time.

There is a video area in the basement and a room in which children can paint and draw or listen to lectures on Greek mythology from their teachers. One useful feature is a free audio guide in a language of your choice, provided you present personal identification or leave a set of house keys at the desk during your tour, to ensure return of the equipment. The villa is interesting but has too many copies for my liking; I prefer the larger **Musée de Béatrice Ephrussi de Rothschild**, which contains lots of authentic paintings, sculptures and fine period French furniture.

Beaulieu has a few nearby features worth viewing. The first is the beautiful Rotonde historic building topped with a dome that allows light to flood in. Now reburbished and retitled **Les Salons de la Rotonde Lenôtre**, it hosts receptions, has an excellent patisserie and boasts its cooking expertise. It is on avenue Fernand Dunan and was used as a hospital for French troops during the Second World War. White plaster cherubs encircle the roof, and inside there is fine plasterwork and a large glass chandelier in the elegant round salon.

The little park beyond the Rotonde has attractive small sculptures nicely situated among the shrubs and trees to enhance the public amenities. Under the trees are three white, life-size marble Venus statues in various states of undress, and across the road there is a bronze sculpture of a little girl with her sand bucket near the strand. A stone plinth nearby with a small bronze relief portrait of a soldier holding his rifle serves as a reminder of the losses at the battle of Verdun in 1916 and carries the proud declaration, 'On Ne Passe Pas'.

The **Villa and Gardens of Ephrussi de Rothschild** were built by Baroness Béatrice Ephrussi de Rothschild during the belle époque period of 1906–12. Béatrice was the daughter of Jewish banker Alphonse de Rothschild. Alphonse was one of five banking brothers who initially lived in Frankfurt in the nineteenth century. The brothers decided to emigrate, each to a different European capital, to extend their business networks and make even more money. Alphonse went to Paris. They financially supported the Alliance in the war against Napoleon, and after the success of that campaign they were made barons by the Austrian emperor. In England the Rothschild dynasty financed the Industrial Revolution and became incomparably prosperous as a result. As their banking business burgeoned, they extended their interests to culture and the arts, and into the wine trade in France, owning the famous Mouton Rothschild and Château Lafitte vineyards. Alphonse de Rothschild formed an art collection with paintings by Rubens, Rembrandt, Vermeer, Watteau, Boucher and Fragonard, and these were part of the household in which his daughter Béatrice grew up in nineteenth-century Paris.

Born in 1864, Béatrice got married at a young age to Baron Maurice Ephrussi, who was an art collector and a businessman of means living in Paris. She travelled widely while he gambled extensively, and eventually he lost all his money, after which she divorced him to protect her name and interests. She was already a rich woman, but soon afterwards became much richer when her father died and left her an immense fortune. She was now in a position to buy whatever she wanted, and she did so with abandon for the rest of her life, indulging her eighteenth-century taste. After buying a villa in Monaco near the famous casino, where she liked to have a flutter, she purchased seventeen acres of land on the picturesque peninsula of Cap Ferrat (Wild Cape) near Beaulieu, and had her pink and white grand Italianate villa constructed there to accommodate her growing collection of old master paintings, sculptures, fine furniture, silk garments and fine porcelain. Giroux was the architect. She also employed the best horticultural talents to create a series of gardens about the villa, and the result was nine exquisite gardens with different themes. The various flowers, shrubs and trees were augmented by columns, waterfalls, ornamental ponds, sculptures and ceramic features to create a wonderland of visual sensation. On completion of the ambitious transformation, she had thirty-five full-time gardeners employed to maintain the property.

The baroness divided her time between Paris, Monaco and Cap Ferrat, using the latter as her winter residence. She continued buying large consignments of antiques in London and Paris and had train-loads transported down to Beaulieu, where they were unloaded for her inspection. The best ones were sent to the new villa on Cap Ferrat and the remainder to her villa in Monte Carlo, or else returned unpurchased. When she eventually died, the villa and its valuable contents were bequeathed in her memory to the **Académie des Beaux-Arts** of the Institut de France. It remains today as it was then, preserved for public benefit for posterity, after a refurbishment in 1991. The house and gardens are still meticulously maintained by a team of experts.

The literature about the villa describes it as containing a priceless collection of Renaissance and eighteenth-century art. I have to express some disappointment and disagreement with that assessment. The baroness lacked really good taste, particularly in paintings. There was a certain vulgarity about the way she spent her money. She was something of a bargain-hunter, rather than a real connoisseur. For example, the 'Tiepolo' ceiling painting which she purchased for her Venetian Rococo room is so patently inferior to the work of that great Venetian master that it could not possibly have been painted by him. The present custodians of the villa no longer claim it as such but merely attribute it to Tiepolo, or as eighteenth-century Venetian. Likewise, many of the fine Italian paintings in the Great Reception Room are without attributions, and some are damaged and in urgent need of restoration. Nowhere is there an absolute masterpiece of the Renaissance period to be seen – though there are very good examples, such as the altarpiece dedicated to Saint Brigid, and the primitive painted portrait of an Italian nobleman. For a collector who sometimes bought works from the noted Wildenstein art dealers of Paris and London, one would have hoped to encounter even greater treasures here. In fairness, the baroness did amass what is probably the largest and finest collection of Vincennes and Sèvres

porcelain in the world. She was obviously an expert in this field. Her taste for oriental silk garments seems to have been very good, and she acquired some superior-quality paintings and drawings by eighteenth-century French masters Boucher and Fragonard, which adorn the reception rooms. Furniture provenance, rather than exceptional quality, seems to have been very important to her. Panelling came from the Hôtel de Crillon in Paris. A carpet used to be on the floor of the Château de Versailles. At least two pieces of exquisite French furniture formerly belonged to Queen Marie-Antoinette. The villa also contains superb Beauvais, Aubusson and Gobelin tapestries and many sculptures and iconic fragments of fine artistic quality, removed from convents and churches after the chaos of the French Revolution.

In summary, Baroness Ephrussi de Rothschild created a sumptuous memorial devoted to art and beauty. The villa is full of interest, and the gardens are simply glorious to experience at all times of the year. She did a most generous thing in bequeathing it to the nation for posterity. The house contains a restaurant where excellent food can be enjoyed by visitors amidst beautiful surroundings and with wonderful views across the bay towards Villefranche. Fountains and strains of classical music will add to the overall enjoyment of a visit.

Cap Ferrat has other attractions for visitors. The poet and all-round man of the arts Jean Cocteau also decorated the Salle des Mariages in the Hôtel De Ville of the nearby port of St-Jean-Cap-Ferrat, as he did in Menton, and it is available for public viewing when not in service. The former fishing village is now a very upmarket residential quarter with a Sotheby's real estate office, catering to millionaire bankers and international art collectors. Some commercial art galleries and exhibition spaces in the village cater for modern tastes. Contemporary sculptures line the seafront, though not all deserve such unrivalled display venues. Nearby, a plaque at place David Niven records that the famous film star once lived there. One tall abstract stainless steel sculpture by an artist named Helidon reflects its surroundings like a mirror and recalls a giant oval reflecting sculpture by British artist Anish Kapoor in a square in Chicago. The more traditional bronze figure of *Kneeling Fisherman* by Claude Vignon stands on a plinth near the seafront where the fishermen used to draw up their boats. Nowadays, the port is crammed with luxury yachts. Nearby is a bronze bust in tribute to the French poet Charles Baudelaire, and on the waterfront is a fine bronze of a *Warrior Spearing a Giant Octopus*, artist unknown.

The little **Église Saint-Jean-Baptiste**, dating from 1793, has a dark interior illuminated by eight attractive stained-glass windows, some of which illustrate the miracles of the loaves and fishes and of Christ changing the water into wine at the marriage feast of Cana. Outside, on the veranda facing the sea, is a monument to the fallen and a bronze relief portrait of General Charles de Gaulle (1890–1970).

It is worth travelling up the twisting road to the top of the hill near the extremity of the cape to visit the **Allied War Cemetery**, where a proud bronze *Cockerel on a Rock* presides over the many graves.

The **Chapelle St-Hospice** beside the graveyard is a historic monument of ancient lineage. Its outstanding feature is the giant bronze sculpture of the *Vierge Noire*, 1903, by the Italian artist Grancillo Galbusieri, which stands beside the little church. It is a monumental eleven metres high and comprises a giant crowned Virgin Mary holding in her arms the infant Jesus, also wearing a crown, and holding symbolic items in his hands. Its sheer size and dark patination inspire reverence and awe. A plaque on the church wall states that it is the place of the Chevaliers de Malte. Inside are old paintings and images showing an abbot about to be beheaded by savage invaders. There are also modern religious paintings by an artist named Marchand Le Roux in the manner of Picasso, and a quite attractive stained-glass window at the entrance, also by Roux. This completes the survey of beautiful Cap Ferrat, a most suitable location to complete a healthy one-hour walk about the Cap, before enjoying delicious seafood luncheon at one of the many excellent restaurants in St-Jean-Cap-Ferrat.

For those interested in seashells, there is a museum of seashells, **Musée des Coquillages**, at quai du Vieux Port.

Mougins

South of France guide books usually recommend a visit to Mougins because of its famous restaurants and excellent food. That may be the case, but there is another good reason one should visit the pretty, concentric hilltop village: the wonderful new privately-owned Mougins **Museum of Classical Art (Musée d'Art Classique de Mougins** or **MACM)** on rue Commandeur, which opened its doors to the public in May 2011. It is a magnificent cultural addition to Mougins.

Mougins is a concentric hilltop town situated midway on the road between Cannes and Grasse. It is best approached by car, though the number 600 bus from Cannes stops at Val de Mougins. From Val de Mougins, the number 23 local bus takes you up the steep 2-kilometre slope to the village or, of course, one can walk.

Mougins village has a long, colourful history. It was occupied by the Romans and was attacked by marauding Saracens over many centuries before they were finally banished from the region. The mayor of the village, Dr Richard Galy, in a preface to a publication marking the opening of MACM, writes that the village has always maintained close links with culture and artists. Francis Picabia built his home there in 1924, and in 1936 Pablo Picasso and his friends Jean Cocteau, Man Ray and Paul Éluard stayed at the Vaste Horizon hotel. Picasso later settled nearby at Mas Notre-Dame-de-Vie, where he died in 1973. Other celebrities who stayed there or in the vicinity include Fernand Léger, Jacques Brel, Edith Piaf and Christian Dior. The trend continues today. Christian Levett of Clive Capital, a London commodities hedge fund founder, purchased a villa there and liked it so much that he decided to build his personal museum in the village. Still relatively youthful, Mr Levett is a born art collector who has amassed over 900 important works in a short space of time. In an interview given to *Apollo Magazine* in February 2011, he stated that he had the collecting bug from the age of five. His initial purchases of Greek and Roman classical art and artefacts were hugely augmented by purchasing practically the entire collection of Berlin collector Axel Guttmann (1944–2001) when it came on the market after his untimely death.

La Lutte de Jacob et de l'Ange 1966 Marc Chagall Oil on canvas

Mr Levett has a passionate interest in classical art and decided to open his own museum in Mougins village, so that others could enjoy the art as much as he does. Mougins won over London, he decided, because the English capital is already well served for museums, and the French Riviera seemed the right place to display his treasures, many of which originated in this historic Mediterranean coastal region.

The collection is rich in Egyptian, Greek and Roman sculpture. It also has a considerable quantity of vases, gold coins and jewellery. One outstanding feature of the museum is the massive collection of ancient arms and armour, in particular a world-class accumulation of bronze helmets. These are objects of considerable beauty as well as having been items of personal protection in the many wars conducted along the coast over the centuries. Especially remarkable is the Corinthian helmet with neck guard and green patina, dating from 650–600 BC.

Mr Levett decided to branch out from the ancient period and collect modern paintings, drawings and sculptures that had a kinship with classicism. Thus, works by Henry Moore, Pablo Picasso, Mark Chagall, Paul Cézanne, Auguste Rodin, Amedeo Modigliani, Peter Paul Rubens and even Andy Warhol, and others, joined the collection. This section is not as strong as the antique sections, simply because the collector has had to confine himself mainly to drawings by some of those famous artists, and one or two drawings are not of the very highest quality. Such gems rarely come on the market these days. He made no mistake, however, in his purchase of the two standing bronze figures titled *Reflection*, 2001, by British artist Antony Gormley (*b.*1950) which stand like sentinels on the wall at the approach to the museum.

Another outstanding recent work is the colourful oil painting of a classical head with damaged nose by Italian artist Carlo Maria Mariani, dated 1998. There are four small portraits of Roman emperors by Peter Paul Rubens, who himself was also an enthusiastic collector. Of the works on paper, the most impressive is the ravishing serigraph by Andy Warhol (1930–87) of the *Birth of Venus*, with flowing golden hair, after the great painting *The Birth of Venus* by Sandro Botticelli (*c.*1446–1510) in the Uffizi Museum in Florence.

The Egyptian section is very strong and contains important sarcophagi and sculptural fragments. A small grey granite head of the eighteenth Dynasty (1361–52 BC) from the young Pharaoh Tutankhamun is outstanding. The Roman section is equally strong and includes some remarkable statues. There are oddities, such as the large carved limestone and marble erect phalluses, said to have been votive objects in ancient times.

To complete his vision for the old and new museum, the collector has also purchased good examples of modern art from the Riviera. In this category are a typical *Venus Blue Torso* by Yves Klein, a *Blue Venus* 2012 in resin by Sacha Sosno, and a bronze *Venus* of 2002 by Arman, all associated with the School of Nice group of artists.

An attractive shop at the entrance has possibly the most expensive postcards on the Riviera at €2 each, but the book on the collection, edited by the curator Dr Mark Merrony, is also available for purchase at €12 for the softcover or €20 for the hardcover edition, and is a real bargain. It is expertly written and copiously illustrated.

After MACM, everything else in the village seems 'small beer'. The Maurice Gottlob (1885–1970) permanent exhibition in the **Espace Culturel** at place du Commandant Lamy is of mild interest, as the artist lived for many years in the area and painted the surrounding landscape with love and attention to detail, even if it was without a truly original talent.

The **Musée de la Photographie** in the imposing restored Saracen stone fort is a pleasure to visit and full of interest. It is the love-child of photographer André Villers (*b.*1930) who knew and shot portraits of the great artists of the region, including Fernand Léger, Alberto Magnelli, Le Corbusier, Salvador Dalí, Hans Hartung, Jean Cocteau and Pablo Picasso. He was a very skilled photographer, as his many fascinating pictures of Picasso attest. It is interesting to see that Picasso liked to paint wearing shorts and a horizontally striped T-shirt, and sometimes without even the T-shirt: in the shot of him painting the *War and Peace* series in Vallauris, he has discarded the shirt and stands in his bare feet on a low stool. We also see that he sketched his outlines with charcoal before beginning to paint.

South of France landscape *c.*1915 Mary Swanzy Oil on canvas

Villers has made most interesting photographic portraits of some of the artists that he got to know. There is a penetrating study of the bearded American artist Paul Jenkins, a pioneer of abstract painting who passed away in 2013 in New York. There are also close-up portraits of Cocteau and Dalí, and a revealing snapshot of French painter Jean-Charles Blais (*b.* 1956) at work.

The photographic exhibitions extend over three floors, and the views from the top windows over Cannes and the green-blue bay are stunning. As in Nice, there is also a most interesting collection of old cameras on display which evoke feelings of nostalgia.

The official tourist brochure for 2014 lists fifteen museums and commercial art galleries in Mougins village that can be visited. Some show what I consider to be tourist art, but a few display works of better than average quality. The old village **Lavoir** in the place de la Mairie is one venue worth a visit. The **Espace Culturel** shows photographs by the gifted Parisian artist Robert Doisneau (1912–94), who has left a legacy of 450,000 negatives and on his deathbed confessed that he had had fun all his life with his camera. The **AE Gallery** shows contemporary art, but the most modern gallery in the village is the white contemporary space owned by artist Sand Breton, who paints in a refreshingly modern abstract manner, preferring subtle nuances of white and grey to a more colourful palette. The **JMG Gallery** specialises in attractive action painting that reminds one of the astonishing drip paintings of the late Jackson Pollock (1912–56). **Galerie Rich Art/Galerie Sintitulo** shows quality work by Arman, Chagall, Miró, Warhol, Sosno and other well-known modern masters. Finally, the **Musée d'Histoire Locale** is worthy of a quick visit to see for yourself the Roman remains and traditional implements that were particular to Mougins over its colourful history.

Visitors will be pleased to learn that the Scottish-born Irish painter Grace Henry, HRHA (1868–1953) visited Mougins at least once and painted what many critics consider her ultimate masterpiece, a glowing study of almond trees in blossom there.

I first heard about pottery from the hill town of Vallauris long before
I got the opportunity to visit. Perhaps because of Picasso's brilliantly
decorated pottery, I expected to see outstanding contemporary ceramic
work still being produced there. Instead I discovered shop after shop
and atelier after atelier producing colourful regional-style pottery
suitable for sale to tourists, and very little of a high aesthetic standard.
My experience was possibly jaundiced because of an initial travelling
mistake. I took the train from Nice and correctly got off at the Golfe
Juan-Vallauris station, thinking I would walk up the two or three
kilometres to the museums and pottery area. It turned out to be an
arduous and dangerous walk in hot sunshine up a steep, winding hill
busy with traffic before I reached the outskirts and encountered
painted ceramic sculptures by Jacotte and Roger Capron. These were
attractive, figurative and colourful, in the manner of Picasso's paintings
of burly bathers in the early decades of the twentieth century. Too late
I discovered local buses passing by that would have brought me
straight to the town centre from Golfe Juan. I made no mistake on the
second visit. One setback of travelling up by the local number 8 or 18
bus service is that you pass by the tourist office on the outskirts of the
town, recently relocated there from a much more central location in
place Paul Isnard beside the church, the museums and the Picasso
bronze sculpture *L'Homme au Mouton*. The bus fare, however, is still
the best value on the Riviera at €1.

Vallauris is another ancient town, dating from as long ago as AD 1138.
It once belonged to the Lérins Abbey on the islands off the coast of
Cannes. The monks encouraged pottery-making because local clays
were suitable for purpose, as in the case of Biot, and the craft was given
a tremendous boost by the influx of Italian potters from Genoa in the
sixteenth century. The trade was petering out in the twentieth century
when Pablo Picasso rented a small villa in the town in 1948 and made
the acquaintance of potters Georges and Suzanne Ramié of the
now-famous **Madoura Pottery**. He encountered other potters there
also, including Adelia Hazama-Rosolen from Nice who showed him
how to throw a pot and work the wheel. With his genius for form it

was not long before he was demonstrating to all at Madoura how to shape and decorate clay in innovative ways to create ceramic works of art that are greatly prized today. He attracted other famous artists to Vallauris to do likewise, including Braque, Cocteau, Miró, Tal-Coat, Chagall, and a host of lesser figures. Suzanne Ramié laughed at Picasso's initial, seemingly clumsy, efforts but soon changed her mind when she realised that he was revolutionising the traditional art form. It was an added bonus when Picasso gave the Ramiés the exclusive right to edition and sell his Madoura ceramics to a world hungry for his art. It made them rich in subsequent years.

The small **Vallauris Museum** is located in the modestly sized château with a courtyard at place de la Libération at the top of avenue Georges Clemenceau. It is beside the impressive **Bibliothèque Municipale**, in front of which stands a towering stone memorial of the Second World War featuring an angel cradling a dead soldier. Various plaques list the names of the citizens who lost their lives in the conflict. The museum contains three separate sections: The **Musée National Picasso** in the little old church off the courtyard, the **Musée de la Céramique**, and the **Musée Magnelli**. These three are well worth a visit. Admission is only €4, or €2 for senior citizens, and gains you access to all three.

Picasso's murals in the **Old Abbey Church** are extraordinary and fascinating to view. I am not sure whether the villagers approached Picasso to paint the smaller inner vaulted room of the deconsecrated church, or vice versa. He had been painting on the damp walls of the Château Grimaldi in Antibes at that time, and may have seized on this second opportunity to paint in fresco. The result was this major double painting sequence, *War and Peace*. Before he could begin to paint, he had to line the damp stone walls with sheets of plywood. When this was done he slapped on a foundation coat and rapidly sketched out his complex figurative compositions in charcoal. After that, it was painting in a frenzy of inspiration. *War* is on the left side, *Peace* on the right. They face each other in amazing contrast. They are joined together at the end wall by four outline figures shaking hands and holding aloft a shield emblazoned with a dove of peace gripping a symbolic sprig of perhaps olive or myrtle in its beak.

The *War* sequence is pregnant with menace and violence. Like an oriental frieze in reverse, the story unfolds from left to right. At the beginning, a guardian soldier stands ready to defend with spear and shield on which the dove image again appears. He is there to repel the rapacious invaders who are cutting, thrusting and chopping the defenders in a murderous black battle scene in the centre of the panel. From the right comes a fearsome charioteer in his chariot drawn by two wild-eyed trampling horses. From one hand he aims a short sword dripping with blood. With his other hand he appears to grip a bag of severed human heads slung over his shoulder, presumably warriors he has defeated and beheaded in battle. His shield is a mass of writhing black scorpion-like insects. Severed hands fall to the ground under the horses' hooves. The overall powerful composition moves from blue and green at the left to grey in the centre and on to green and a mass of bloody brown at the right.

The *Peace* is the complete opposite, an idyllic scene. Pan plays his pipes at the left beside a child who plays with a birdcage on a string, while a little owl crouches on his head (Picasso discovered this pet owl in Antibes). In the centre of the panel two happy naked females dance for joy to the piper's music. Birds fly overhead, while from the right a burly Pegasus horse approaches followed by a happy boy. The horse's face appears to resemble Picasso's, particularly his wide brown Spanish eyes. The final scene on the far right is a tranquil seated group of two naked women and one man in a *Déjeuner sur l'Herbe* scene. One woman breastfeeds her child; the other cooks a meal over a fire. Overhead, the sun bursts through the clouds, illuminating an abundance of oranges and grapes growing among the trees. The whole scene is painted in cream colours against a tranquil background of light Mediterranean blue.

War and Peace is a flawed masterpiece. It does not quite reach the great achievement of *Guernica*, but it nearly does. The only aspect slightly pulling it down is the end wall of the outline black, yellow, red and white people joining hands across the globe in unity, where the execution reminds me of a bland International Labour Day poster. The artist may have rushed this finale after the adrenalin-draining tussle with war and peace. The installation remains, nevertheless, a magnificent achievement.

179

The Salle Alberto Magnelli (1888–1971) is on the top floor of the château. This Italian artist was a lovely colourist and a pioneer of abstract painting in the early twentieth century. In the experimental painting of 1914, *La Japonaise*, he achieves an interesting synthesis of representation and abstraction. There is even a hint of cubism in this subtly coloured portrait of a Japanese woman wearing her kimono, attended by her faithful white cat. He developed from that through collage to vividly-coloured geometric abstraction in the 1950s–60s. The wonderful red and blue geometric abstract canvases of 1969 titled *Overtures No. 1* and *No. 2* suggest he had a love of music also. A single grey sculpture dated 1914 and titled *Rythme Profil* accompanies the paintings and drawings in the permanent collection, some of which were donated by Susi Magnelli, the artist's widow.

The second floor contains a selection of ceramics from the permanent collection of the Ceramics Museum. The decorated pots, jugs and plates of Picasso are out on their own for attractiveness and sheer quality. A large plate constructed in silver relief and numbered 14 from an edition of 20 by him, titled *Visage Géométrique*, is particularly beautiful and innovative, and recalls his Keys painting on the wall of the Grimaldi Castle in Antibes, before it became the Musée Picasso. There are other fine ceramics in the permanent collection by Josep Llorens Artigas and the Massier family. In 2014 Fondation Maeght celebrated its fiftieth birthday by lending further ceramic masterworks from the family collection to Vallauris. These included plates by Braque, Chagall and Miró, as well as abstractions by Chillida, Tal-Coat and Francois Fiedler.

The Vallauris Museum outdoors is surrounded by decorated figurative sculptures by husband and wife ceramic artists, the Caprons, and the works extend to a nearby public park.

The nineteenth-century Madoura Pottery building in the village centre is now an exhibition space. In 2014, it featured the extensive modern ceramic art collection of Parisians Jacques and Benedicte Wattel. Titled *Mission Céramique,* the exhibition focused on French ceramics of the 1950s and 1960s. Stand-out artists featured were Roger Capron (1922–2006), Robert Picault (1919–95) and Francine Delpierre (1917–68). The latter's grey vase of subtle perfection was a highlight in the fine exhibition. Also included were three Aubusson tapestries. Roger Bezombes's (1913–74) theme was *The Coming of the Magi*, woven, 1948–50. The more recent ones were by the acclaimed Sainte-Jean painter Gérard Garouste (*b.* 1946) and his wife Elizabeth Garouste (*b.* 1949), and titled *Les Bulles.* The latter two were created with assistance from Martha Bonetti (*b.* 1952).

The bronze sculpture by Picasso, standing on a plinth in the town square, was gifted by the artist to the townspeople *c.* 1951. It could not be truly described as beautiful, though it is certainly powerfully realised. The man has somewhat skinny legs, and the sheep he holds in his hands looks absolutely terrified. For those reasons it is hardly a self-portrait, though there is a facial resemblance. I suppose every artist puts something of himself into every work.

The **Église Sainte-Anne** of 1839 commands the square and looks down into the ceramic-pot-lined avenue Georges Clemenceau. The façade is richly decorated and has statues in enclaves. Inside it has undistinguished colourful stained-glass windows and Victorian-style religious paintings. Most impressive are the relief sculptures for the Stations of the Cross, by an unacknowledged artist.

Returning by bus to the railway station, visitors will notice an elegant tall narrow stone column in memory of Napoleon in Golfe Juan.

A visit to the pretty Alpine village of La Turbie is worthwhile for several reasons, foremost among them to see and experience the massive *Trophy of Augustus* dominating the village since Roman times. Another reason is that the village has wonderful bird's-eye views of the Riviera and in particular of Monaco. But it also has two interesting churches, one very old and one relatively new, and the core of the ancient village with its portals and narrow, stepped streets is still intact and interesting to explore. For example, there is a remarkable stone fountain with Roman inscriptions in the centre of the village, topped by a substantial urn still in perfect working order. Passing cyclists refill their water bottles from its source. The final reason, and a good one, is that the village has a superior culinary tradition, and an excellent lunch may be enjoyed there.

La Turbie skyline

The ideal way to visit these Alpine villages is by car, but drivers should be warned that the roads are at times narrow and tortuously twisting, and such an undertaking is not for the faint-hearted. If you don't wish to go by car, take the tram from place Masséna in the centre of Nice to the Nice-Vauban bus terminal on the northern outskirts, and board the number 16 bus for Peille village. The second last stop on the route is La Turbie. Buses to and from these villages are infrequent, and you need to obtain a timetable in advance from the tourist office to plan your itinerary with any success.

The *Trophy of Augustus* and **Église Saint-Michel Archange de la Turbie** tower over the village. Before investigating them it is interesting to walk to the nearby **Square Albert Gastaut** to view the war memorial sited in a tiny, well-kept garden. A modestly sized bronze Archangel Saint Michael spears a rather ugly devil with curling tail pinned down beneath his feet. The sculpture is by Greta Alessio and commemorates the many villagers who died for France in the wars. **Place Théodore de Banville** is beside the garden, and the

French dramatist and poet is remembered with a verse from one of his poems on a wall beside the row of restaurants. De Banville (1823–91) was from Moulins in Allier in the Auvergne and died in Paris, but spent time in Nice and La Turbie dreaming about ancient nymphs and satyrs which peopled his romantic poetry.

The tiny **Chapelle Saint-Jean**, beside the seventeenth-century Gioffredo Gate, is the first interesting building you will come across in the ancient quarter. It is no longer open to visitors, but it is possible to peer in through windows in the old door to see a painting of St John over the altar of the single-nave church. The building obviously dates from primitive times. It was cared for by the Pénitents Blancs until the nineteenth century, when they ceased their activities there. It remains fully furnished, which suggests that mass is still sometimes celebrated there.

The larger Église Saint-Michel Archange de la Turbie is very near the older church, and seems to have taken over its functions. It was built by architect Antonio Spinelli in 1764–77 in the Nice baroque style, using blocks of stone taken from the massive nearby ruined Roman Trophy at that time. It is a magnificent church with a coloured-tile exterior cupola and an abundance of fine-veined red marble cladding in the interior. Six attractive side-chapels are each decorated with three antique paintings of good quality, though one has suffered severe damage from dampness. Once again, a large canvas of *St Michael the Archangel Spearing the Devil* hangs over the ornate altar, and it is particularly fine. The Stations of the Cross, antique small painted ovals, are pretty and most unusual. There are also paintings of Saint Charles, Saint Joseph, the Blessed Virgin, the Souls in Purgatory, a powerful Deposition and a Pietà that were obviously painted by skilled artists. They have been variously attributed to Raphael, Rembrandt, Veronese, Brea, Murillo and Ribera in the past, but I have grave doubts about some of these

War memorial at Square Albert Gastaut, La Turbie

attributions. It is possible that a few were copies made after those great artists in the eighteenth century. The church is meticulously maintained and is part of the Parish of Monaco further down in the valley.

The narrow streets of the ancient quarter are lined with massive ceramic jars, probably originally made to store olive oil, as in Vallauris and Biot. Here, they now contain shrubs, trees and flowers, including lemon trees, olive trees, oleanders, hydrangeas and a variety of ferns, though the relative absence of sunlight in these shady areas is not conducive to blooming florescence. The ancient road to Italy, the Via Julia, is still intact and runs straight through the ancient quarter to the thirteenth-century Portal de Réduit and on to the *Trophy of Augustus*, now enclosed by fencing.

Stone fountain with Roman inscriptions in the centre of La Turbie   185

The *Trophy of Augustus* celebrates the victory of Augustus Caesar, the Roman emperor, over the many tribes of the Alps who were finally subjugated by the Romans between 25 and 14 BC. In 7–6 BC the Senate and people of Rome dedicated this great trophy to him. It was erected at the Col de la Turbie, the highest point on the via Julia, so that the emperor could look over all of the French Riviera to his front, and look back to Italy from the rear. Slabs of limestone were cut and hauled from a nearby quarry, and finest white marble was transported from Carrara. It is said that the bodies and arms of the Gauls slain in the various battles were piled up on the site of the trophy in the

traditional Roman manner before construction began, and much of
the building was carried out by prisoners and slaves. The design was
spectacular, based on classical Vitruvian concepts of the square, circle,
triangles and a pinnacle, atop which stood a gigantic statue of the
god-like Augustus pointing his finger towards France and Great
Britain, still to be conquered. It was originally reckoned to be 117 feet
(40 metres) high. Today, it is somewhat less than that, but still over
100 feet (36 metres) tall, despite the ravages of time and its repeated
despoliation, before its partial restoration as a historic monument in
the twentieth century. Its glory ended in AD 476 after the fall of the
Roman Empire. The only other such trophy to survive is apparently in
Romania, although the base of an even older one has been discovered
recently at Le Perthus on the Spanish border.

*Today you enter the enclosed grounds of the Trophy through a
souvenir shop gate at which an attendant charges an admission fee
of €5.50, with no reduction for senior citizens, though there is a
special deal for people under the age of 25 years.*

The surrounding grounds have been planted with appropriate trees,
shrubs and wild flowers, mainly olive or yellow in colour. Wild goats
scamper on precipitous tracks outside of the fence. There are excellent
viewing areas from which you may look down on Monaco nestling in
the steep incline by the blue sea, with extensive views towards the
Italian and French Rivieras. Many blue swimming pools gleam
underneath in the sunshine, attached to the luxury villas of suburban
Monaco on the slopes of the mountain.

The Trophy itself is still magnificent in its partially restored state.
It can be climbed to a considerable height with the permission of the
attendant, and I recommend it, though not for people suffering from
vertigo. Nearby, a small museum building displays a plaster moulding
of the statue of Augustus, a bronze casting of which is now housed in
the Vatican Museum in Rome. It also contains a three-dimensional
model of the Trophy showing the beauty and intricacy of its
architecture and the many statues, columns and relief carvings that
once adorned it. Two great friezes still survive on the French-facing

side of the Trophy itself. The museum also shows a video, made in 2011, of the history of its reconstruction and restoration, and displays many fragments which remain unattached.

Jean-Camille Formigé (1845–1926) and his son Jules Formigé (1879–1960) were the architects in charge of the restoration. It was a fifty-year dream, made possible by an American millionaire named Edward Tuck who paid for most of it. Prince Albert I of Monaco also assisted. Tuck's wife, Julia Stell (1850–1928), was a confirmed Francophile and chose to live out the rest of her life in France rather than in America. A philanthropist, she gave a sumptuous collection of objets d'art to the Musée du Petit Palais in Paris, and gave the Domaine de Bois–Préau to the Musées Nationaux so that it became part of the Musée de la Malmaison. Recently, further renovation was carried out on the Trophy in 2011, paid for by the Stavros Niarchos Foundation and other parties.

I have dealt at length with the great Trophy of Augustus because I consider it a supreme example of an architectural work of art, worthy of an art lover's visit. Outside of the enclosed area, the village authorities have erected a viewing platform, 'Le Rondo', from which visitors have an unrivalled panoramic view over Monaco and the capes on either side, jutting out into the blue sea. On a nearby hill gleams the white dome of an observatory. Butterflies abound among the wild flowers. Dante Alighieri mentioned the village in the Purgatory section of *The Divine Comedy*. It remains a special place without much changes after a few thousand years.

Peille is a tiny historic village perched on the side of the mountains, some six or seven kilometres further on from La Turbie. The number 116 bus journeys on to it, and has to negotiate very narrow roads and three tunnels through rocks in which there are literally only inches to spare for the doughty bus driver. The horn must sound frequently, to warn possible on-comers and avoid collisions. Along the way, one passes the enormous quarry of La Turbie, still in use since Roman times. At the bottom of a steep ravine is a large cement factory.

Apart from these two incursions on nature, the scenery is still wild and awesome. At the approach to the village you can see a Monument to the Fallen on top of a high rock. Two ruined castles are in evidence, one of them a **Palais de Lascaris**. The inhabitants still speak their own dialect, and live in a series of steep medieval streets leading down to the Paillon River which flows on to L'Escarène, another hill town. This was the ancient salt route from Nice to Turin in olden days. The attractive seventeenth-century neoclassical stone church of **St-Pierre-aux-Liens,** with its distinctive square bell tower, stands on the hill behind a modern inn. It was designed by Jean-André Guibert, the architect of the Cathédrale St-Réparate in the old town of Nice. It is not open to the public daily, but can be opened on request.

Peillon is a similar tiny village on an adjacent hill. It is best approached by car, as it does not have a regular bus service. Both villages are connected by a most interesting hikers' path. The baroque Church of the Transfiguration is at the top of the village. The main attraction for art lovers is the **Chapelle des Pénitents Blancs**, which is decorated with a series of Renaissance frescoes on the *Passion of Christ* by the distinguished fifteenth-century artist–priest of the region, Giovanni Canavesio (1450–1500).

Jean or Giovanni Canavesio was born in Pinerlo, Piedmont, Italy in 1450 and became a Catholic priest, with religious painting as his special talent. He was in demand as an artist on the French side of the Alps in the fifteenth century, and many churches were decorated by him. Perhaps his masterpiece is in the church of **Notre-Dame-des-Fontaines**, a few kilometres away from La Brigue near the Italian border. The entire walls of the interior of the church were frescoed by Canavesio, depicting the *Passion of Christ*. One art critic determined that the priest exhibited an anti-Semitic note in these paintings, blaming the Jews for the torture and crucifixion of Christ. The artist's frescoes were also particularly graphic in underlining aspects of sin and the temptations of the devil, who was depicted as an ugly horror. The gifted artist–priest died comparatively unknown outside of the Alpes-Maritimes region. Entry to the church must be arranged through the local tourist office.

Menton

The palm-lined seaside town of Menton, famed for its gardens and production of lemons, lies within walking distance of the Italian border. Its near-subtropical climate enticed many nineteenth-century European royal and wealthy families to establish winter residences there. The Irish painter Louis le Brocquy (1916–2012) and his artist wife Anne Madden (*b.* 1932) lived near Carros village in the Alpes-Maritimes for many years before returning to reside in Dublin. Le Brocquy once told an invited audience that his first glimpse of Menton from the sea completely enthralled him. He had never before seen such a beautiful sight of magnificent buildings situated in such a glorious landscape, all shimmering in the noonday heat of the Mediterranean coast. He and his wife decided at that moment to settle in the south of France and establish their atelier there near Carros village. There is enough good art to see there to justify the visit.

The number 100 bus from the terminus beside MAMAC and the Louis Nucéra Library in Nice will take you to Menton for the standard fare of €1.50, which applies to any destination on the Riviera. It takes almost an hour and a half to travel by this means, but it is well worth it: the views of the sea and mountains en route are spectacular. The train journey is quicker, if you are impatient, but you would miss some entrancing views.

The **Musée des Beaux-Arts** in Carnolès on the outskirts of Menton is the first suggested stop. Alight from the bus at the Pont de l'Union roundabout, which is graced by a carved female sculpture titled *Déesse de la Musique*, by artist Albert Douillon. The museum is just across the road from the roundabout. The building is rather splendid, even if the collection of art inside is something of a disappointment. It used to be known as Le Palais Carnolès, again built by the Grimaldis in the eighteenth century, after which it fell on harder times. In 1969 it was classified as an historic monument, and in 1977 it became the Musée des Beaux-Arts or Museum of Fine Arts, largely as a result of a substantial donation of old and modern works of art by the collector Charles Wakefield Mori, who lived in the vicinity. There were other donations, but not many and not of particularly fine quality, apart from a large canvas of 1966 by the fine English modernist painter Graham Sutherland (1903–80). Sutherland lived part of every year in Castellar near Menton, in a house purchased from the famous designer/architect Eileen Gray, from 1947 until his death in 1980. The title of his gift is *The Fountain*; it is predominantly red, but not one of his very best works. He is perhaps best remembered for his portrait of the writer Somerset Maugham, in which he captured in minute detail the lizard-like features of that talented curmudgeon, and for his harrowing portrait of Winston Churchill, which was destroyed by Churchill's widow after his death. The museum charges an entrance fee of €2.

In the permanent collection there is a tolerable St-Tropez *Landscape*, 1918, by Moïse Kisling, and a competent red and blue abstraction titled *Composition*, 1966, by the Russian School of Paris artist Serge Poliakoff (1900–69), which won the Grand Prix of the sixth Biennale of Menton in 1966. The synthetic cubist artist Albert Gleizes (1881–1953), who was mentor to modernist Irish artists Evie Hone and Mainie Jellett, is represented by a fine large rotational composition of 1932 titled *Support de Contemplation*. One of the best modern paintings in the collection is the large canvas *Vénus Noire*, 1919, by Suzanne Valadon (1865–1925).

The upstairs rooms have a number of pieces of sculpture, including the impressive bronze bust of a dancer by Jean-Baptiste Carpeaux (1827–75). Most of the others are by Riga-born Léopold Bernstamm (1859–1939), who came to live in Menton. His life-size plaster cast of a standing female nude seems better than the many conventional portrait busts there. One room has a large Gobelin tapestry hanging on a wall. It was woven in the seventeenth century, after the painter Charles le Brun. The downstairs rooms are used mainly for temporary exhibitions.

The new **Musée Jean Cocteau**, largely featuring the collection of Cocteau's work by Séverin Wunderman, is the main museum to visit in Menton. It charges an entrance fee of €6 to €8. Located at the end of the promenade on quai Monléon, and facing the Bay of Garavan, it is a magnificent new building designed imaginatively by French architect

Rudy Ricciotti to house the collection. It was inaugurated in 2011 by Frédéric Mitterrand, then Minister for Culture and Communications.

The architect won the competition in 2007 from eighty-two submissions, and lost no time in designing and constructing the lovely, light-filled building, which is proving to be a very special tourist attraction for Menton. He describes it as follows: 'My museum is fluid like Cocteau's line: low, white, powerful and sensual. It is built in concrete and glass on a triangular plan, and it opens onto an extensive forecourt where, set into the ground, is a characteristic pebble sculpture of a lizard by Cocteau. By night, when the museum is lit up, it looks like a gathering of racing yachts, or flowing locks of hair'.

Inside the building, the permanent collections are on two floors, and at the entrance a large area is set aside for temporary exhibitions. There is also a smart coffee dock area and a well-stocked souvenir and bookshop.

Jean Cocteau (1889–1963) was something of an enigma. He was born at Maison-Lafitte and grew up in Paris of a nervous disposition. He began to draw at an early age and grew to enjoy cinema and the circus. In 1898 his father committed suicide. Cocteau was a mediocre student at school but soon ran away to Marseilles, where he began to write poems and continued to draw feverishly. He went on to have a very successful social and artistic life, becoming friends with Picasso and Matisse, as well as composers Stravinsky, Milhaud, Satie and others, and became involved with the Russian Ballet Company, then resident in Monte Carlo. He had his poems published, and illustrated books of other poets, before turning in earnest to drawing, oil painting, ceramics, and tapestry design. In 1953 he had an exhibition of his creations at the Galerie des Ponchettes in Nice. He was elected a Chevalier of the Legion of Honour, and was subsequently elected to membership of the French Academy in 1955, a great honour. He was a restless artist, travelling extensively and making several classic films.

In 1956 Cocteau commenced decorating the interior of the tiny chapel of St Pierre in Villefranche, and persuaded the authorities in Menton to allow him to paint the walls and ceiling of the **Wedding Room**

The new *Musée Jean Cocteau* at Menton

beside the town hall. His final major initiative was to persuade the
Menton authorities to convert the 1610 ancient seafront defence
structure known as the Bastion into a Cocteau Museum. He donated
paintings, pastels and ceramics to the museum, and in 1961 he
designed a giant mosaic made of pebbles from the beach, featuring
a lizard that would symbolise, in his own words, that 'fine
Mediterranean idleness' and would also make him immortal. He also
designed three attractive mosaics that today adorn the façade of the
Bastion Museum, which continues to open to the public like the new
Cocteau Museum only a few hundred metres away. Cocteau died in
1963 of a heart attack.

Jean Cocteau grew to love the French Riviera and left his mark on
many parts of it. He was lucky that a Parisian jeweller and watchmaker
named Séverin Wunderman began to collect his work in 1950 and
over the subsequent sixty years amassed nearly a thousand books,
drawings, paintings, jewellery and ceramics by the artist. Having
moved the collection to California and exhibited it there, Wunderman
decided to donate it to Menton in the artist's memory, which is how
the new museum came into being. It is a marvellous story of artist and
devoted collector making something special happen.

Entrance to the *Bastion Museum*

Visitors should experience both the new museum and the old museum in the Bastion, if they have the time. The Wedding Room is also open to the public on weekdays and is a good example of Cocteau as a draughtsman, at his best. He was not a great painter like Picasso and Matisse, but his ceramics and drawings held up well to the works of those great masters of modern art in the show that featured the three of them at the new museum in 2014.

The town of Menton has many buildings of architectural distinction to enjoy as one meanders through the streets full of historic interest. The cathedral and various churches can be visited at certain times. Saint-Michel, the largest, is a most ornate baroque building of the seventeenth century. The town has also many sculptures worth viewing dotted about in public places.

The figurative bronze sculpture of *Ulysses* on a marble plinth out on the point, dated 2004 by Czech artist Anna Chromy, (*b.* 1940) is eye-catching. So too is the carved sandstone *Reclining Venus* by local artist Volti on the central avenue de Verdun, where the annual spring celebratory carnival of the citrons is held. La Fête du Citron takes place in February and features enormous wire-framed sculptures and lemon-adorned floats and is a festival to be much enjoyed. Also along that avenue is the impressive **Palais de l'Europe**, which has a fine exhibition space for displaying art. Some years ago it featured two hundred examples of beautiful textile artefacts known as Molas made by the Cuna Indian women of the San Blas Islands off the coasts of Panama and Colombia in Central America. These colourful, ingenious abstract and representational appliqués came from a Paris private collection, and the exhibition was accompanied by a handsome scholarly publication on that ancient art form.

Mirrors should think longer before they reflect.

Jean Cocteau

Ultra-fashionable St-Tropez is a most pretty town of fun and character on the Golfe de St-Tropez further down the coast from Cannes and Fréjus. It is not so convenient to get to from Nice: there is no direct train or bus service. A much better idea is to take a day trip (at approximately €60 per person) from the port of Nice on a comfortable tourist boat. Before berthing in the Nouveau Port at St-Tropez, it will call briefly to les Îles de Lérins off the coast at Cannes, and pass by the Esterel, a massive red rock coastline. There is time to briefly explore this glamourous tourist Mecca, including a walk around the crammed outdoor shaded food and textile market, take lunch, visit the town's superb little museum of modern art, and get back to the port for the return journey to Nice – all in all an exhilarating experience.

The **Musée de l'Annonciade** on rue Georges Clemenceau is the best thing in the town for art lovers. It possesses a stunning collection of early twentieth-century Fauve paintings by some of the greatest French artists of the twentieth century. It is said that the wealthy post-impressionist from Paris, Paul Signac (1863–1935) first discovered it as a desirable place to paint when he sailed into St-Tropez in 1892, and liked it so much that he bought a villa and invited his band of artist friends of the Fauve (wild beast) movement to join him.

These artists, known at that time as the wild beasts of colour and freedom of expression, included de Vlaminck, Derain, Braque, Matisse, Vuillard, Bonnard, Van Dongen, Friesz, Cross, Marquet and Dufy, and they all came to visit and paint there for a time. Through the good offices of Signac, the town ended up getting an enviable collection of avant-garde art at a time when it was not yet appreciated for how good it was. The Fauve movement centred at Collioure near the Spanish border at l'Estaque and at St-Tropez. The collection was first housed in a cramped room in the town hall, known as the Museon Tropelen, until after the Second World War when the ruined and neglected chapel of the Pénitents Blancs was restored and refurbished as a museum to house the valuable collection, where it remains today. It is one of the art highlights of the extended French Riviera.

It is difficult to pick out favourites, so good is the overall collection. One of the best-known paintings, on loan from Paris and formerly owned by Signac, is *Luxe, calme et volupté* of 1905 by Matisse, which features frolicking nude bathers for which St-Tropez beaches became famous. It is a pointillist blaze of colour and innovation. Matisse's painting of *La Gitane*, dated 1906, is ravishingly beautiful, and to use Bernard Berenson's oft-quoted aphorism 'life-enhancing'. André Derain (1880–1954) is represented by two of his most famous paintings, the views of *Waterloo Bridge* (1906) and *Westminster Palace* (1907) in London, which Derain visited at that time at the suggestion of the art dealer Ambrose Vollard. No British painter had ever portrayed the capital city of England in such glowing colours as the visiting French artist. There is a small but delightful early canvas by Georges Seurat (1859–1891) titled *Canal de Gravelines* dated 1890.

Seurat died tragically young, having demonstrated unique originality and vision and had an especially strong influence on Signac with whom, amongst others, he founded the Société des Artistes Indépendants.

200   *Westminster Palace* 1907 André Derain Oil on canvas

Braque's painting here is *Paysage de l'Estaque*, another masterpiece to rival Bonnard's luscious romantic *Nu devant la cheminée*. Albert Marquet (1875–1947) habitually painted seascapes further down the coast at the Ile de Porquerolles, and he is represented by a scene that is above his usual standard, in keeping with the high standards of his more famous colleagues.

The same could be said for the pointillist Henri-Edmond Cross (1856–1910) and for Raoul Dufy (1877–1953), both of whom also rose to the challenge. All of these lovely paintings hang on the ground floor of the little museum, and to experience them is to feel great joy.

Paysage de l'Estaque 1906 Georges Braque Oil on canvas

Upstairs there are a number of splendid bronze sculptures of corpulent nudes and portrait busts by the important sculptor Aristide Maillol (1861–1944) and a few other works by lesser-known artists. Maillol's *La Nymphe*, opposite, features on the cover of this guide.

If you have time and the inclination, a gentle stroll around the town will reveal other things of interest. There is a statue of Admiral Suffren on a pedestal looking out over the old port, near the now defunct **Château de Suffren**. There are two churches to visit, **Église de St-Tropez** on rue de la Ponche and **Chapelle de la Miséricorde** on rue Gambetta. The town hall still holds occasional art exhibitions of artists living locally, but the standard is uneven and can be a disappointment.

Celebrated in song by Pink Floyd, St-Tropez is probably best known internationally for the many film stars and fashion models that find their way down there after the Cannes Film Festival. Unsurprisingly, Brigitte Bardot lived there for a time. The 1956 film *Et Dieu Créa la Femme* directed by Roger Vadim was shot in St-Tropez and starred Brigitte Bardot and is generally credited with catapulting the then peaceful fishing village into the international spotlight.

French writers Guy de Maupassant, Françoise Sagan and Jean-Paul Sartre have spent time there. Jack Nicholson and Robert De Niro have been photographed there, mixing with the beautiful, the rich and the many thousands of 'lion-hunters' who flock there every summer in the hope of catching a glimpse of such celebrities. I wonder if many of them venture into the little **Musée de l'Annonciade** to catch a glimpse of the real treasure of beautiful St-Tropez.

St-Tropez continued and still continues to attract artists over the years, including Bernard Buffet (1928–99), Irish artist Mary Swanzy HRHA (1882–1978), who resided there for eighteen months, Italian artist Massimo Campigli (1895–1971) and the famous Irish architect–designer Eileen Gray (1878–1976) lived there for a time and designed a villa on the outskirts of the resort. Today, German artist, Stefan Szczęsny (*b.* 1951) continues this tradition.

La Nymphe 1931 Aristide Maillol Bronze

Draguignan may be the final town of the French Riviera region of the Var, depending on who you talk to about the extent of the Riviera. Since the arrival of the Artillery School in 1976, the previously small town has developed into a city. **Le Musée Municipal** is a little gem of a museum. It occupies an old Ursuline convent that was converted into the local fine art museum as far back as 1888. It occupies only four or five rooms on the ground floor, but four of these are laden with treasures. Ancient ceramics, Roman glass, antique armour, marble busts and plaster fauns and satyrs keep company with a collection of antique paintings, many of which are of outstanding importance.

Pride of place goes to the great Dutch master Rembrandt van Rijn (1606–69), whose small half-length oil portrait of a rosy-cheeked boy holding a glass bowl in his hands is a true delight. The boy wears an elaborate hat, and a gold chain and medallion hang about his neck. The picture is beautifully painted and is in remarkably good condition for its obvious age. It is a penetrating study of profound insight, yet of great simplicity and economy of focus. It came from the famed Château de Vintimille, which has to be a very good provenance.

Could it be a portrait of the artist's beloved son, Titus, who died young? Possibly not. Wisely, the authorities display it behind a glass panel for protection. It is a painting on canvas without a frame and is unsigned, though the attribution to Rembrandt is justified.

Draguignan is 80 km from Nice. It proves a bit of a drag to get to the town of the dragons, if you will forgive the pun. Unless you wish to drive there, I found that an early morning Paris-bound train from Nice got me to Arc-Draguignan Gare in one and a quarter hours. Alas, the town of Draguignan is a further ten kilometres away from Arc, where St Joan of Arc was once active, but a number 5 bus eventually got me there after a circuitous route for the modest sum of €1. It was worth the trouble and expense, if only to visit the little Musée Municipal on the rue de la République, a narrow side street off the main thoroughfare, where you will also find the tourist office.

The next noteworthy picture is Renoir's affectionate portrait of a baby with red cheeks and wearing a white bonnet. It is just possible that this is a portrait of his son Coco as an infant. It is simply adorable. Renoir's romantic brushwork is as magical as ever, and the colours are subtle and seductive. There is a very good landscape by the lesser-known French impressionist Charles Camoin (1879–1965) titled *Naples, Le Vésuve, vu de la Villa Capella*, 1904, showing an attractive pink and yellow villa to one side of a distant view of the heavenly blue sea and low, dark hills seen from a luxuriant Côte d'Azur garden.

Many of the paintings in the collection are understandably given attributions, since their histories have probably been lost over the centuries. I like to think that the vivid *Head of Christ*, wearing the crown of thorns, attributed to the splendid French painter Philippe de Champaigne (1602–74), is accurate. Likewise, the two small oil panels of aristocratic lovers in a garden, and attributed to the great Peter Paul Rubens (1577–1640), are probably, in my judgement, by that artist.

There is a charming pastel double portrait by François Boucher (1703–70) of a man teaching a girl how to play the flute. Another outstanding French picture is the *Head of a Young Woman* by Jean-Baptiste Greuze (1725–1805), who was wont to paint pictures of young girls in trouble. Likewise impressive is the half-length portrait of the *Countess of Provence*, Marie Joséphine de Savoie, elegantly dressed and holding a pink rose in her hand. The painting is attributed to the artist François-Hubert Drouais (1727–75), a Parisian painter of the aristocracy.

Amédée Van Loo (1719–95) is represented by two oil paintings of ladies seated at their sewing and spinning activities. Finally, of the many fine French paintings on display, there is the large *Death of Cleopatra* by Jean-François De Troy (1679–1752), an artist I seldom come across in art museums and sale catalogues.

The collection also contains good Italian and Flemish paintings. Giovanni Paolo Panini's (1691–1765) elaborate interior of St Peter's Basilica in Rome is most impressive, and typical of his architectural oeuvre. David Teniers the Younger (1610–90) is represented by two archeytypal peasant village scenes. In one a crowd of villagers loiter about a kitchen eating and smoking. In the other, the doctor is attending to a patient by letting his blood, a favourite Flemish artistic theme. A number of other paintings of quality are to be seen in this museum, as well as many interesting sculptures. A small white marble carving of a *Woman Sitting by the Fire*, by Camille Claudel (1864–1943), is most competent and charming. Antoine-Denis Chaudet (1763–1810) has sculpted a strong bust of Napoleon in white marble, which is also in the collection. The finest of the lot is the marble bust of *Comte de Valbelle* by Jean-Antoine Houdon (1741–1828), who really captures the personality as well as a probable likeness of a French aristocrat.

If that is not enough to please you, then make sure to look closely at the ancient ceramics from Roman and Gallo-Roman times. There are very lovely ancient shapes and forms to be compared and contrasted with later Sèvres, Rouen, Moustiers, Marseilles and Delftware plates, plus Syrian, Egyptian, Indian, Palestinian and Anatolian unglazed ceramics donated by a regional collector. The museum also contains pieces of fine furniture. On one occasion I visited, the front room was given over to the works of a contemporary local artist where the standard was unworthy of the excellent museum.

Pierre de la Fée dolmen in Draguignan   207

The old town is interesting to explore. I recommend a walk to the
Tour de l'Horloge at the top of the town, which is open to visitors.
It can be climbed to the top and offers outstanding views on all sides.
It is also used as an exhibition space for contemporary art. Beside it is
the **Théâtre de Verdure**, and then the no-longer used twelfth and
thirteenth century small **Chapelle Saint-Sauveur**. The more modern
Parish Church of St Michael, near the town centre, is worth a visit to

enjoy the many colourful stained-glass windows honouring various saints. It contains not just one but two statues of St Michael slaying the dragon. Its finest artistic feature, however, is the frieze of four large antique religious paintings hanging over the altar. One of them, *The Visitation*, is attributed to Charles Van Loo; the other three are by anonymous artists. There is a particularly fine set of stained-glass panels at the rear of the church, admitting brilliant light over the organ loft.

Not too far away, you will encounter the **Musée des Arts et Traditions Populaires**, off rue Joseph Roumanille. It has displays of old agricultural machinery in the forecourt, and a small outdoor garden growing roses and vines of the region. Entry is free to the ground floor display, but there is a charge of €3.50 for a conducted tour of the ethnographic collection housed upstairs.

I had had enough of art for one day, but was pleased to come across a large mural on an outside wall of a nearby building beside the rue des Jardins. The busy composition of local landmarks featured the famous *Pierre de la Fée* dolmen, the Tour l'Horloge, and the Église with its soaring steeple near some trees, flowering irises and a view of nearby hills. The artist even included the Dragon blazon of the town in a fine panorama that is fresh and typical of Provence.

Colour is all.

When colour is right,

form is right.

Marc Chagall

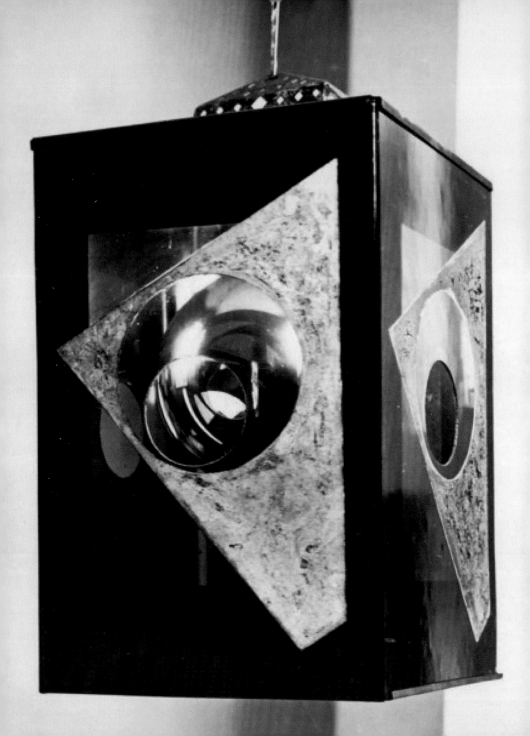

Èze is an ancient hilltop village dating from as far back as the Bronze Age. Phoenicians, Turks, Saracens, Italians, Greeks and of course French invaded this outpost, until it was finally ceded to France by Italy in 1860.

The hilltop village of Èze

A most alluring bronze sculpture of a naked nymph entitled *Kohinoor* by sculptor Amaryllis Bataille greets you as you alight at the village bus stop. She is an enchantress with a fishtail and bears the name of a famous diamond. The baroque church of the **White Penitents Chapel**, built in 1764, towers over the village. It contains interesting artefacts and works of art, including an Egyptian cross and a painting titled *The Day of Doom*, showing the flames of hell scorching the sinners on earth. Above and behind it is the oldest surviving church, the **Chapel of Saint-Croix**, built in 1306 under the care of the Pénitents Blancs. It contains exceptional antique furnishings and a painting of the Crucifixion, attributed to Louis Brea.

Èze village is 429 metres high and has extraordinary, exhilarating views of the French Riviera from the arid exotic garden and ruined tower at its summit. Two ancient châteaux still remain, well-maintained and in constant use. **Château Eza** was for a time the residence of Prince William of Sweden and is now a complex of artists' studios, restaurants and shops. The exclusive **Château de la Chèvre d'Or** is a most elegant hotel with an art collection and Michelin-starred fine dining restaurants. Perhaps the most impressive sculpture is that of a life-size bronze crusader on horseback, brandishing a gleaming brass shield,

The number 82 bus from Vaubon station in Nice gets you to Èze village, in 35 minutes. The views of mountain valleys and sparkling sea along the way are simply enthralling.

which dominates the car park. The extensive terraced gardens contain bronzes of various animals, including gilded lions, a golden goat, a giraffe and a rearing horse, as well as numerous carved marble male and female figures, often antique. Those lucky enough to lunch at the garden restaurant Les Ramparts will enjoy superb French cuisine at international prices. They will also have an unrivalled bird's eye view of Cap Ferrat nestling down below in the azure sea with countless sundry yachts, motor boats and larger liners criss-crossing the placid expanse of sparkling water. They may rub shoulders with writer Philippa Gregory, actor Sean Connery or Bono of *U2*, all of whom frequent this venue. This château received its name from a wild goat which is said to have led ancient invaders to their doom on the steep rocks while they clambered up to try to capture the château.

The hilltop village is full of interest to art lovers and shoppers looking for attractive souvenirs. The narrow paths wind up and down the hill, and there are architectural features of interest at every turn. There is a small **Musée-Salle d'Expositions** where contemporary art is exhibited from time to time. On the way back down, one passes **Sentier Friedrich-Nietzsche**, a challenging steep track winding down through the tree-clad steep gorge to sea-level at Èze-sur-Mer,

View of Cap Ferrat from the restaurant *La Chèvre d'Or*, Èze

which can be negotiated by fit people in approximately one hour.
Athletes tend to go down and back up again in under two hours.
The philosopher Nietzsche is said to have done it regularly and
found there his inspiration for *Thus Spoke Zarathustra*.

There is a tourist office beside the front square, in which there is
a regular outdoor market of jewellery, food and textiles. Finally, for
those seeking perfumes and aromatic soaps there is a Fragonard
factory shop nearby and a rival Galimard outlet with elegant displays.
Èze is a treat to visit.

Coaraze is another attractive hilltop village, though it is best
approached by car. The nearby **Saint-Sébastien Chapel** was adorned
with mural paintings in the sixteenth century, but only some of them
survive. The rear wall has a fine depiction of Saint-Sébastien, riddled
with arrows, by an anonymous sixteenth-century artist. Some
nineteenth-century alterations have damaged the painting.

The mountain village of **Lucéram** is dominated by **Sainte-
Marguerite Church**, which is the main artistic attraction. It was
built at the end of the fifteenth century in a Romanesque-Gothic
style and renovated in the seventeenth century. The artist–priest
Canavesio painted five impressive panels there in the fifteenth
century, including images of Saint Anthony of Padua. The Nice
artist Louis or Ludovico Brea contributed no fewer than ten panels
on the life of Saint Margaret, probably around the same time. The
church also contains precious gold and silver plate in the tabernacle.

The church of **Notre-Dame-de-Bon-Coeur**, some two kilometres
away in the direction of Col Saint-Roch, is decorated with frescoes by
the fifteenth-century artist Jean Baleison, about whom little is known.
These deal with the life of Christ and the Blessed Virgin.

Another tiny chapel, one kilometre south of Lucéram, dedicated to
Saint Grat, was also painted by Jean Baleison, who may have been
a priest, like Canavesio. The theme again is that of the Madonna
and Child.

Falicon is another tiny village, perched on a hilltop. The local **Benedictine Abbey Church** was rebuilt in the seventeenth century and has antique and modern frescoes and other religious artefacts.

Aspremont is a picturesque hilltop village built in concentric circles like Saint-Paul. The local church has decorations and an attractive polychromed statue of the Virgin and Child.

Contes was a fortified village in the past. The parish church has an exceptional panel painting dedicated to Saint Mary Magdalene and attributed to the famous Brea brothers.

Tourette-sur-Loup was also a fortified town in the mountains. Its fifteenth-century church has work by the Brea brothers and a Gallo-Roman altar dedicated to Mercury, the messenger of the gods. The **Chapelle St-Jean** at the entrance to the village has modern frescoes painted by Ralph Soupault in 1959.

A few kilometres away the **Château Notre-Dame des Fleurs**, a nineteenth-century castle built on an eleventh-century Benedictine Abbey, is now a modern art gallery containing works by Arman, César, Warhol and others. Viewing is by appointment only. **Atelier Saez** on route de Saint-Jean shows contemporary art.

The ancient town **Fréjus,** of Roman origin, beyond Cannes is not noted for art – apart from its churches, which are worth visiting. The **Cathédrale St-Léonce** in place Formigé has massive carved doors and inside has a Retable de Saint-Marguerite, (*c.* 1450), by Jacques Durandi, a lesser-known artist from the ancient School of Nice.

In the **Tour de la Mare** district of Fréjus is the octagonal chapel of Notre-Dame de Jerusalem, now better known as the **Cocteau Chapel**. It was designed by the artist, who made detailed plans for its interior decoration but unfortunately died before he could carry them out. In the end the authorities contacted Cocteau's former partner and heir, Édouard Dermit, who was also an artist. He painted the interior wall in the manner of Cocteau, with frescoes featuring likenesses of

Cocteau's friends the Weisweillers, and a former lover, Jean Morais, depicted as an angel. The result is satisfying, if not as vivid or authentic as the little St Peter's Church in Villefranche.

The medieval village of **Roquebrune** near Menton clings to the hillside, and its winding streets lead up to an ancient château built in the tenth century by the counts of Ventimiglia. It was modified in the fifteenth century and had a succession of owners over the intervening centuries before it became the property of the local citizens.

The **Church of Sainte-Marguerite,** dating from the twelfth century, stands on rue du Château. It underwent modifications in later years and contains an inspiring painting of the seventeenth century, titled *Resurrection and Pietà*, by little-known local artist Marc-Antoine Otto. The villagers still hold a colourful annual religious procession in honour of the Virgin Mary. Many celebrities have visited the pretty village over the years, and some have decided to retire there. Perhaps the most famous is the great Irish poet William Butler Yeats (1865–1939), who died and was buried there. His remains were later disinterred and returned to Ireland on the instructions of the Irish government, and reinterred in Drumcliffe churchyard in County Sligo. The tombstone over his grave there carries his immortal words: *Cast a cold eye / On life, on death. Horseman, pass by*.

There is still some controversy over where exactly the great lyric poet was buried in Roquebrune graveyard, and whether or not the correct bones were later disinterred after the Second World War and brought home to Ireland with great fanfare for a state funeral. In any event the poet's immortal words will be remembered forever.

Cap Martin is a little peninsula next to historic Roquebrune, connected by a walking track to both Menton and Monaco, and is now one of the most expensive and fashionable areas on the French Riviera in which to reside. It was not always so. It must have been relatively inexpensive when the Irish architect and innovative furniture designer, Eileen Gray (1878–1976) purchased a site there in 1926 and built the beautiful, futuristic villa on the Cap, known as *E 1027* for herself and her

Romanian lover and fellow architect Jean Badovici in which to reside.
The site was isolated with wonderful views overlooking the grey-
white rocks, the blue Mediterranean and Monaco in the distance.
The enigmatic title *E 1027* is a coded amalgam of their initials. Their
relationship cooled down or ceased after a few years and Gray moved
away from the sea to the picturesque hilltop town of Castellar nearby
where she purchased another site at 187 rue Castellar in 1932–34.
There she designed and had built another futuristic geometric villa in
which to reside. She named this second villa ***Tempe a Pailla***.
Ownership of *E 1027* seems to have passed to Badovici by this stage.
They remained good friends, however. The second villa was occupied
and looted during World War Two as was *E 1027*. She later had it
restored and in 1954 sold it to the English painter Graham Sutherland
(1903–1980) and his wife. The Sutherlands maintained it as a
summer residence.

But Eileen Gray was not finished with her love affair with the French
Riviera yet. Her last purchase was an abandoned stone structure in a
small vineyard on the outskirts of of the artistic colony of St-Tropez in
1939, the year of the start of the terrible Second World War.
She was at this stage seventy-six years old but her vigour was

undiminished. She transformed the crumbling house and added a
wing to it, naming it **Lou Pérou** in memory of a fascinating visit in her
youth to that exotic South American country of the Incas. The garage
of the house had a flat roof, and it was her special pleasure to spend
the evenings seated on that roof watching the sun set over the French
Riviera in all its kaleidoscopic fiery splendour. She died in Paris in
1976 at the age of ninety-seven years, at a time when her reputation
was beginning to be recognised. Today she is regarded as one of the
most original and innovative designer/architects of the twentieth
century. Universities and international museums vie to collect and
exhibit her futuristic furniture. Art historian Dr Jennifer Goff has
written her biography, and the late novelist, Maeve Binchy, met her
in London at a Victoria and Albert Museum Celebration Exhibition
a few months before Eileen Gray died. Her vivid account of that
meeting was published in the *Irish Times* newspaper in January 1979.

Sadly, Gray's masterpiece *E 1027* did not fare well after she left it.
Before the war, Badovici and Gray were friendly with the celebrated
Swiss-French architect Charles-Édouard Jeanneret-Gris (1887–1965)
better known as Le Corbusier, who was also an accomplished painter.
Le Corbusier had stayed at *E 1027* and admired the purist architecture

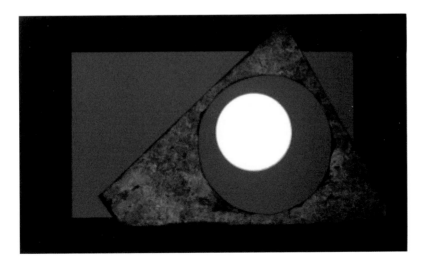

Monte Carlo Lantern 1923 Eileen Gray Glass and metal

of Gray's villa *E 1027*, but convinced Badovici that it could be lightened up and enhanced by the addition of interior colourful murals. He got permission to paint these in 1938–39, and the figurative compositions may have alluded obliquely to Gray's bisexuality. Gray found out about the murals and was furious. She considered it a desecration of her quiet, sacred space, and tackled Le Corbusier about it, but he remained unrepentant and wished to have his murals photographed for posterity. They were never friends thereafter, though she remained on good terms with Badovici until his death from cancer in Monaco in 1956, after which she arranged his funeral affairs.

After World War Two, the villa became the property of Nice artisan, Thomas Rebutato, and he built l'Étoile de Mer, a bar restaurant beside *E 1017* in 1949. Le Corbusier advised and painted the murals on it also. In 1950, Le Corbusier had acquired a site near *E 1027* on which he built a *Cabanon de Vacances* for himself. His final involvement with the site was to design a set of five innovative holiday cabins known as *Unités de Camping* built between 1951–1957, behind and slightly to the right of *E 1027*, crowding its space.

Le Corbusier loved the tiny architectural complex, and it was his delight to dwell in his small cabonon and descend by a narrow path to swim in the sea. He suffered a heart attack and drowned while swimming there in 1965 and was buried with his wife in a pre-planned tomb in Roquebrune churchyard. His cabin still survives near the coastal track, which is now known as promenade Le Corbusier, and there is a bronze bust of him on the **Sentier Littoral** by Arlette Somazzi. After years of neglect, *E 1027* along with the adjoining structures has been restored and donated to Conservatoire de Littoral at Cap Moderne. Each summer from 1 May to 31 October the compact complex is open, by prior appointment, for two-hour group visits. The most satisfactory way to visit is by rail to Gare de Roquebrune Cap-Martin from which it is a short walk to the fenced-in site which is only partly visible from the rocks below.

A visit to the *E 1027* villa is a pilgrimage for lovers of exceptional modern architecture. It may be that Gray was a more imaginative avant-garde architect than her more famous fellow-architect Le Corbusier, who is rightly lauded as a giant of twentieth century design. Yet, his massive revolutionary communal building on stilts or pilotes at Marseilles of 1951 now seems outdated and has not aged well, unlike Gray's magical villa which retains an eternal charm and pared-down beauty. Despite her significance, Gray is quite invisible on the site apart from a plaque on the small entrance gate which reads 'Association Eileen Gray. l'Étoile de Mer. Le Corbusier.'

The one-hour coastal walk from the villa around the Cap to Carnolès is recommended. Broom, myrtle, olive, pine and agave grow in profusion and the honeyed sea air is most bracing.

Gray was relatively well off and could afford a number of residences in her lifetime. She was born near Enniscorthy Ireland in 1878, the daughter of wealthy artist James MacLaren Smith and her aristocratic Scottish mother, soon to become Baroness Lady Gray. Educated in fine art at the Slade School of Art in London, she travelled extensively to Paris to design avant-garde furniture and objets d'art. She opened a sales outlet, **Jean Desert**, in Paris in 1922 and it continued in business until 1930. Her initial design success was a Boudoir Bedroom for Monte Carlo in 1923. It included rugs and lacquer furniture and was exhibited in 1925 at the Exposition des Arts Décoratifs et Industriels Modernes in Paris. But perhaps the most successful piece of furniture of her entire career was the minimal Adjustable Table of 1925, made of chromium-plated tubular steel and glass, which is nowadays mass-produced and an international seller to the sophisticated. Architecture ultimately became her abiding passion.

The large city of **Toulon**, famous today for its rugby, was a Roman colony before it was integrated into France in the fifteenth century. It is regarded as the western end of the Côte d'Azur, which starts at its eastern end at the border with Italy. Toulon's main museum is **Maison de la Photographie** at rue Nicholas Laugier. It has a high-quality collection by master photographers of the twentieth century, and also shows contemporary paintings and sculpture on a regular basis. The city has excellent bus, train and ferry services, and there is an international airport at neighbouring Hyères. The **Musée de la Marine** at place Monsenergue has a collection of ships, models and historic paintings of the city.

Conclusion

The Côte d'Azur is the closest I have come to paradise during this existence. My work entailed a great deal of travel about the globe, including living for extended periods in beautiful regions in Asia, Africa and the Americas. Yet, for me, the south of France beats them all for overall attraction, since it possesses so many interesting things to see and do that the others do not.

Orange and lemon trees grow in profusion and seem to keep fruiting throughout the four seasons. The air is constantly scented from the multiplicity of perfumed flowers that thrive in the semi-tropical climate, giving rise to a thriving perfume industry centred at Grasse. Birdsong is widespread along the coastal strips, and even the bees have a variety of flowers and flowering shrubs and trees to choose their nectar from in the valleys. As a result, you can choose from Acacia honey, wildflower honey or even the stronger chestnut honey to enjoy with your morning croissant and tea or coffee.

There is an abundance of gourmet meals to be experienced in the many restaurants that exemplify famous French cuisine. There are no fewer than 25 Michelin-starred restaurants, including the famous 3-star Le Louis XV-Alain Ducasse in Monte Carlo. Fresh fruits of the finest quality are available all year round from the adjoining regions. It is even said that there are more than ninety different varieties of tomato grown in the Riviera, as well as rarities such as truffles, and of course there are the great vineyards and wines of the region. It has a wonderful climate, and the spectacular coastal scenery makes bathing in the sea, walking in the Alpes-Maritimes or simply strolling about the streets such an enduring and enjoyable experience.

And then, importantly, as I hope I have illustrated in this guide, there is the art to enjoy.

It was no wonder that the great modern artist Pablo Picasso left Málaga for Paris and ended up in the Côte d'Azur, where the beaches and the presence of so many beautiful young women inspired him to create some of the most wonderful paintings and sculptures of the twentieth century. He lived around Antibes and Cannes before ending his days near Mougins. You can enjoy some of the most awe-inspiring examples of his revolutionary art in the great Musée Picasso in Antibes. Likewise, another leading figure in modern art, Henri Matisse, came from northern France to the sunny Riviera on the advice of his doctor because he suffered from bronchitis. He was so excited and inspired by the unique light reflected off the blue sea in the Bay of Angels at Nice that he stayed there more or less for the rest of his long life. He left the Rosary Chapel in Vence as his last enduring masterpiece for all who are interested to go and see.

Pierre-Auguste Renoir, another great modern master, migrated south in old age on the advice of his doctor. He bought a villa above Cagnes-sur-Mer with an olive grove and a heavenly view of the sea and the Château Grimaldi in the distance. The shock of such enduring beauty inspired him to turn to sculpture with the help of skilled assistants, and he has left us a legacy of glorious bronze female sculptures in the garden of his former home, which is now a national museum. Visitors also have the privilege of seeing Chagall's epic biblical scenes in the amazing eponymously named museum in Nice, as well as Legér's masterpieces at Biot.

There is an abundance of art treasures in this beautiful region, as I hope I have outlined in this book. With great satisfaction I note that the treasures are not confined to the past: the French Riviera continues to be a vibrant and exciting arts environment.

There is the new Musée Bonnard at Le Cannet, the new Musée Jean Cocteau at Menton, the new Villa Paloma and Villa Sauber in Monaco, the new Musée d'Art Classique de Mougins and the recently established Gottfried Honegger l'Espace de l'Art Concret in Mouans-Sartoux. All of these are great artistic additions to the cultural richness which exists throughout the region.

Artists still flock to the coast. Not all will become famous, but some probably will in the years to come, when posterity makes the judgement. I accept that it is very difficult to decide what is excellent in contemporary art, and all of us may make judgements that turn out to be spurious. This should not inhibit us from admiring and enjoying what we really like.

My wife and I came under the spell of the magical French Riviera many years ago after a few business trips to the region and some later vacations at lovely Tourrettes-sur-Loup and Juan-les-Pins. The spell is still upon us, and we get increasing pleasure from visiting and revisiting our many favourite places and discovering new favourite places. I hope, after reading this guide, that you will also feel persuaded to share our obsession and plunge happily into the great art to be experienced on the French Riviera.

Useful information on art venues

Every effort has been made to ensure the accuracy of this information, however, the detail is liable to change so it is advisable to get updated information if planning a visit. Most of the venues close on 25th Dec; 1st Jan, 1st May and other public holidays.

A

Acropolis Conference Centre
esplanade J F Kennedy BP4083, 06302 Nice
T +33 (0)4 93 92 83 00
www.nice-acropolis.com

Anatole Jakovsky International Museum of Naïve Art
Château Sainte-Hélène, 23 avenue de Fabron 06200 Nice
T +33 (0)4 93 71 78 33
www.nice-tourism.com
Free Entry Closed Tues

Ancien Forum de l'Urbanisme
place Pierre Gautier – 06300 Nice
T +33 (0)4 97 13 24 82
Closed Tues Open daily 8 am – 6 pm

Archaeological Museum and Roman Excavations of Cemenelum
160 rue des Arènes, 06000 Nice
T +33 (0)4 93 81 59 57
Closed Tues Open daily 8 am – 6 pm

Atelier Rifaldi Gallery
4 rue Sainte-Réparate (Vieux Nice) 06300 Nice
T +33 (0)4 93 85 56 97
www.rifaldi.com
Open Mon - Fri 9 am – 12 pm / 2 – 6 pm
Sat by appointment

B

Barbary Villa
2 carriero Fernand Barbary 06510 Carros
T +33 (0)4 93 08 72 59
Closed Sun & Mon 10am – 12.30pm / 2 – 5.30pm (6pm May, June, Sept)
July & Aug: Closed Mon 10am -12.30pm / 2 – 6.30pm

Basilica Notre-Dame
37 avenue Jean Médicin 06000 Nice
T +33 (0)4 93 88 73 63
Open 8.30 – 12 noon / 2 pm – 7 pm

Bastion Museum
quai Napoléon III, Bastion du Vieux Port 06500 Menton
T +33 (0)4 93 57 72 30
www.tourisme-menton.fr
Closed Tues Open 10 am – 12 noon / 2 – 6 pm

Boisgirard & Associates
40-42 rue Gioffredo 06000 Nice
T +33 (4) 93 80 04 03
www.boisgirardpca.auction.fr
Open Tues – Fri. 7:30 am – 12:30 pm / 2.30 pm – 6.30 pm

C

Casino de Monte Carlo
place du Casino 98000 Monaco
T +377 98 06 21 21
www.casinomontecarlo.com
Open daily from 2 pm

Cathédrale Saint-Réparate (Nice Cathedral)
3 place Rossetti 06300 Nice
T +33 (0)4 93 92 01 35
www.cathedrale-nice.fr/sainte-reparate
Closed Mon Sun 9 am – 1 pm / 3 – 6 pm
Open 9 am – 12 noon / 2 pm – 6 pm

Centre d'Art la Malmaison
47 boulevard de la Croisette 06400 Cannes
T +33 (0)4 97 06 44 90
Closed Mon Open 10 am – 1 pm / 2 – 6 pm

Centre International d'Art Contemporain
(CIAC) place du Château 06510 Carros
T +33 (0)4 93 29 37 97
www.ciac-carros.fr
Free Entry Closed Mon
Open 10 am – 12.30 pm and 2.30 – 5.30 pm
(Open to 6.30 pm Jul & Aug)

Chagall Museum
avenue du Docteur Ménard 06000 Nice
T +33 (0)4 93 53 87 20
www.musee-chagall.fr
Closed Tues
Open 8 am – 5 pm (6 pm May - Oct)

Chapelle de la Miséricorde
cours Saleya 06300 Nice
T +33 4 92 00 41 90

Chapelle des Pénitents Blancs (Folon Chapel)
Centre Ville, St-Paul de Vence
T +33 (0)4 93 32 68 04

Chapelle du Rosaire (Matisse Chapel)
466 avenue Henri Matisse 06141 Vence
T +33 (0)4 93 58 03 26
Closed Fri and Sun
Open Tues & Thur 10 – 11.30 am / 2 – 5.30 pm
Open Mon & Wed 2 – 5.30 pm

Chapelle du Saint-Sépulchre
place Garibaldi 06300 Nice.
e stsepulcre@gmail.com
Open Tues afternoon 3 – 5.30 pm

Chapelle de la Très-Sainte Trinité et du Saint-Suaire (Holy Trinity and Holy Shroud Chapel)
1 rue du Saint Suaire, Nice
www.penitents-rouges.org

Chapelle Notre-Dame-de-Jérusalem (Cocteau Chapel)
route de Cannes 83600 Fréjus
T +33 (0)4 94 53 27 06
www.frenchriviera-tourism.com
Closed Mon Open 9.30am – 12.30 pm / 2 pm – 6 pm (Apr – Sept)
Closed Sun & Mon Open 9.30am – 12 noon / 2 pm – 4.30 pm (Oct – Mar)

Chapelle Sainte-Croix
2 rue Saint-Joseph 06300 Nice
T +33 (0)4 9385 43 45
www.penitents.blancs@wanadoo.fr

Chapelle Saint-Pierre - Chapelle Cocteau
Villefranche-sur-Mer
www.villefranche-sur-mer.org
Closed Tues and mid-Nov – mid-Dec
Open 10 am – 12 noon / 3 – 6 pm (Apr – Sep)
10 am – 12 noon / 2 – 6 pm (Oct - Mar)

Château de la Chèvre d'Or
rue du Barri, 06260 Èze Village
T +33 (0)4 92 10 66 66
www.chevredor.com

Château de Mouans
see Espace de l'Art Concret

Château Eza
rue de la Pise, 06360 Èze Village
T +33 (0)4 93 41 12 24
www.chateaueza.com

Château Grimaldi
place Grimaldi 06800 Cagnes-sur-Mer
T +33 (0)4 92 02 47 35

Château-Musée Grimaldi
Haut-de-Cagnes - place du Château 06800
Cagnes-sur-Mer
www.cagnes-tourisme.com
T +33 (0)4 92 02 47 35
Closed Tues
Open 10 am – 1 pm / 2 – 6 pm (Jul & Aug)
10 am – 12 noon / 2 – 5 pm (Oct – Mar)
10 am – 12 noon / 2 – 6 pm (remainder of year)

Cocteau
See Chapelle Notre Dame de Jerusalem,
Chapelle Saint-Pierre & Musée Jean Cocteau

D

Darkroom Galerie
12 rue Maccarani 06000 Nice
T +33 (0)4 93 76 74 59
www.darkroomgalerie.fr

E

E 1027 (Villa of Eileen Gray)
06190 Roquebrune-Cap-Martin
T +33 (0)6 48 72 90 53
www.capmoderne.com/fr
Reservation required
e contact@capmoderne.com

Église Notre-Dame de l'Annonciation
1 rue de la Poissonnerie 06359 Nice
T +33 (0)4 93 62 13 62
Open daily 7 am – 12 pm and 2.30 pm – 6 pm
Sun 8 am – 12 pm and 3 pm – 6 pm

Église Sainte-Jeanne d'Arc
86 avenue Saint-Lambert 06100 Nice
T +33 (0)4 93 84 54 60

Espace a Vendre
10 rue Assalit 06000 Nice
T + 33 (0)9 80 92 49 23
www.espace-avendre.com
Closed Sun & Mon   Open 2 – 7 pm

Espace de l'Art Concret
Château de Mouans
13 place Suzanne de Villeneuve
F06370 Mouans-Sartoux
T + 33 (0)4 93 75 71 50
www.espacedelartconcret.fr
July & Aug open daily 11 am – 7 pm
Sept – June open Wed – Sun 1 – 6 pm
Closed 25 Dec – 1st Jan

Espace Soardi
9 avenue Désambrois 06000 Nice
T +33 (0)4 93 62 32 03
www.soardi.fr
Closed Sun & Mon

F

Fondation Émile-Hugues
2 place du Frêne 06140 Vence
T +33 (0)4 93 58 15 78
www.vence-tourisme.com
Closed Mon Open 11 am – 6 pm

Fondation Ephrussi de Rothschild
06230 Saint-Jean-Cap-Ferrat
T + 33 (0)4 93 01 33 09
www.villa-ephrussi.com
Open daily 10 am – 6 pm (7 pm July & Aug)
Nov - Jan Mon– Fri 2 – 6 pm /
Sat & Sun 10 am – 6 pm

Fondation Hartung-Bergman
173 chemin du Valbosquet
F-06600 Antibes
T +33 (0)4 93 33 45 92
www.fondationhartungbergman.fr
Open Fri at 2 pm (Apr – Oct)
Reservation required

Fondation Maeght
623 chemin des Gardettes 06570
St-Paul de Vence, France
T +33 (0)4 93 32 81 63
www.fondation-maeght.com
Open daily 10 am – 6 pm

Fragonard
see Musée Fragonard & Villa-Musée
Jean-Honoré Fragonard

Franciscan Museum of Cimiez
place du Monastère 06000 Nice
T +33 (0)4 93 81 00 04
www.nice-tourism.com
Free Entry Closed Sun
Open 10 am – 12 noon/ 3 – 6 pm

G

Galerie de Cannes
111 rue d'Antibes 06400 Cannes
T +33 (0)4 93 99 07 92
www.galeriedecannes.com

Galerie Catherine Issert
2 route des Serres 06570 St-Paul de Vence
T +33 (0)4 93 32 96 92
www.galerie-issert.com

Galerie Céramique du Château
45 rue du Château 56400 Auray
T +33 (0)2 97 50 72 88

Galerie Chave
13 rue Henri Isnard 06140 Vence
T +33 (0)4 93 58 03 45
www.galeriechave.com

Galerie Depardieu
6 rue docteur Jacques Guidoni 06000 Nice
T +33 (0) 966 890 274
www.galerie-depardieu.com
Closed Sun Open 2.30 pm – 6.30 pm

Galerie des Dominicains
9 rue Saint-François de Paule 06300 Nice
T +33 (0) 966 890 274
www.lesdominicains.com

Galerie d'Hercule
see Grimaldi Palace, Monaco

Galerie des Ponchettes et de la Marine
59 & 77 quai des Etats-Unis 06300 Nice
T + 33 (0)4 93 62 31 24
Closed Mon

Galerie du Temple
12 rue Maccarani 06000 Nice
T +33 (0)4 93 27 04 97
www.galeriedutemplenice.com

Galerie Ferrero
2 - 6 rue du Congrès 06000 Nice
T + 33 (0)4 93 88 34 44
www.galerieferrero.com
Closed Sun Mon - Thurs 2 – 6.30 pm
Fri & Sat 10 am- 12.30 pm / 2 – 6.30 pm

Galerie Gantois
56 rue Grande 06570 Saint-Paul de Vence
T +33 (0)4 93 32 01 55
www.galerie-gantois.com
Open 10 am – 7 pm

Galerie Golconda
rue Place de la Grande Fontaine
06570 Saint-Paul de Vence
T +33 (0)4 93 32 51 73
www.galeriegolconda.com

Galerie Hurtebize
Le Grey d'Albion, 17 La Croisette
06400 Cannes
T +33 (0)4 93 39 86 84
www.galerie-hurtebize.com

Galerie l'Art Vivant
51 rue Saint-Pierre 89450 Vézelay
T +33 (0)3 86 40 98 50

Galerie Lapita
1 place Charles Félix, cours Saleya
06300 Nice
T +33 (0)9 81 41 95 69
www.galerie-lapita.com

Galerie le Capricorne
64 rue Grande 06570 Saint-Paul de Vence
T +33 (0)4 93 58 34 42
www.galeriecapricorne.com

Galerie Maud Barral
16 quai des Docks 06300 Nice
T + 33 (0)7 86 34 37 50
www.galerie-maud-barral.com

Galerie Sapone
25 boulevard Victor Hugo 06000 Nice
T +33 (0)4 93 88 54 27
www.saponegalerie.com
By appointment

Goetz-Boumeester Museum
La Citadelle 06320 Villefranche-sur-Mer
T +33 (0)4 93 76 33 27

Grimaldi Forum
10 avenue Princess Grace 98000 Monaco
T +377 93 25 18 31
www.grimaldiforum.com

Grimaldi Palace
98015 Monaco
T +377 93 25 18 31
www.palais.mc
Open 10am — 6pm

H
Hierro Desvilles Art Gallery
4 rue Antoine Gautier 06300 Nice
T + 33 (0)4 97 12 15 15
www.hierrodesvillesartgallery.com

Holy Trinity Church
11 rue de la Buffa 06000 Nice
T +33 (0)4 93 87 19 83
www.anglican-nice.com

Hôtel Windsor
11 rue Dalpozzo 06000 Nice
T +33 (0)4 93 88 59 35
www.hotelwindsornice.com

L
La Colombe d'Or Hotel
06570 St-Paul de Vence
T +33 (4) 93 32 80 02
www.la-colombe-dor.com

La Grande Bibliothèque Louis Nucéra
2 place Yves Klein 06000 Nice
T +33 (0)4 97 13 48 00 / 48 90
Closed Mon Sun 8 am – 6 pm (2 - 6 pm Oct - Jun)
Open Tues Wed 8 am – 7 pm Thurs – Fri 2 – 7 pm

Librarie-Galerie Matarasso
2 rue Longchamp 06000 Nice
T +33 (0)4 93 87 74 55
www.laure-matarasso.com
Closed Sun & Mon
Open 8 am – 12.30pm /4 – 7.30 pm

M
Maeght Foundation *see Fondation Maeght*

Maison de la Photographie
rue Nicholas Laugier 83000 Toulon
T +33 (0)4 94 93 07 59
www.toulon.fr
Closed Sun & Mon. Open 12 noon – 6 pm

Masséna Museum
65 rue de France & 35, promenade des Anglais
06000 Nice
T +33 (0)4 94 93 07 59 *Closed Tues*

Matisse Chapel *see Chapelle du Rosaire*

Musée Bonnard
16 boulevard Sadi Carnot 06110 Le Cannet
T +33 (0)4 93 94 06 06
www.museebonnard.fr
Closed Mon Open 10 am – 6 pm

Musée Château
Château Sainte-Hélène, 23 avenue de Fabron
06200 Nice
T +33 (0)4 93 71 78 33

Musée de l'Annonciade
rue Georges Clemenceau 83990 St-Tropez
T +33 (0)4 94 17 84 10
ww.saint-tropez.fr
Closed Tues Open 10 am – 1 pm / 2 – 6 pm

Musée d'Art Classique de Mougins (MACM)
32 rue du Commandeur 06250 Mougins
T +33 (0)4 93 75 18 22
www.mouginsmusee.com
Open 10 am – 12.30 pm / 2 – 6 pm

Musée d'Art et d'Histoire de Provence (MAHP)
2 rue Mirabeau, Grasse
T +33 (0)4 93 36 80 20
www.museesdegrasse.com
Free entry Open 10 am – 5.30 pm (7 pm May - Sept)

Musée de Béatrice Ephrussi de Rothschild
see Fondation Ephrussi de Rothschild

Musée de la Castre
Le Suquet, rue de la Castre 06400 Cannes
T +33 (0)4 89 82 26 26
Closed Mon Open 10 am – 1 pm / 2 – 5 pm

Musée de la Céramique
rue de la Fontaine 06220 Vallauris
T +33 (0)4 93 64 71 83
www.vallauris-golfe-juan.fr

Musée de la Chapelle de la Visitation
placel de la Visitation, Monaco-Ville 98000 Monaco
T +377 93 50 07 00
Closed Mon. Open 10am - 4pm

Musée de la Photographie
67 rue de l'Église 06250 Mougins
T +33 (0)4 93 75 85 67
Closed Mon Open 10 am – 12.30 pm / 2 – 7 pm

Musée des Beaux-Arts (Museum of Fine Arts)
33 avenue des Baumettes 06000 Nice
T +33 (0)4 92 15 28 28
www.musee-beaux-arts-nice.org
Closed Mon

Musée des Beaux-Arts du Palais de Carnolès
3 avenue de la Madone, Palais Carnolès, Menton
T +33 (0)4 93 35 49 71
www.villedementon.com
Closed Tues

Musée d'Histoire et de Céramique Biotoises
9 rue Saint-Sébastien 06410 Biot
T +33 (0)4 93 65 54 54
www.musee-de-biot.fr

Musée Fragonard
14 rue Jean Ossola 06130 Grasse
T +33 (0)4 93 36 02 07
www.fragonard.com
Free entry Closed Sun in Nov, Jan and early Feb
Open 10 am – 6 pm (7 pm in Jul & Aug)

Musée Jean Cocteau
2 quai de Monléon, Menton
T +33 (0)4 89 81 52 50
www.museecocteaumenton.fr

Musée Magnelli
place de la Libération 06220 Vallauris
T +33 (0)4 93 64 71 83
www.vallauris-golfe-juan.com

Musée Matisse
164 avenue des Arènes de Cimiez 06000 Nice
T + 33 (0)4 93 81 08 08
www.musee-matisse-nice.org
Closed Tues

Musée Municipal d'Art et d'Histoire
9 rue de la République 83300 Draguignan
T +33 (0)4 98 10 26 85
www.ville.draguignan.fr

Musée Municipal de Mougins - Espace culturel
place du Commandant Lamy 06250 Mougins
T + 33 (0)4 92 92 50 42

Musée National Fernand Léger
316 chemin du Val de Pôme 06410 Biot
T +33 (0) 4 92 91 50 30
www.musee-fernandleger.fr
Closed Tues Open 10am - 5pm (6 pm May - Oct)

Musée National Picasso
place de la Libération 06220 Vallauris
T +33 (0)4 93 64 71 83
www.musee-picasso-vallauris.fr
Closed Tues   Open 10am – 12.15pm / 2 – 5pm

Musée Renoir
19 chemin des Collettes 06800 Cagnes-sur-Mer
T + 33 (0)4 93 20 61 07
Closed Tues
Open: 10 am – 12 noon / 2 – 6 pm (Apr & May)
10 am – 1 pm / 2 – 6 pm (June - Sept)
10 am – 12 noon / 2 – 5 pm (Oct - Mar)

Museum of Asian Arts
405 promenade des Anglais Arènas
06200 Nice
T +33 (0)4 92 29 37 00
www.arts-asiatiques.com
Free Entry Closed Tues

**Museum of Modern and Contemporary Art /
Musée d'Art Moderne et d'Art Contemporain**
(MAMAC)
promenade des Arts 06000 - 06300 Nice
T + 33 (0)4 97 13 42 01
www.mamac-nice.org
Closed Mon Open 10 am – 6 pm

N
Negresco Hotel
37 promenade des Anglais 06000 Nice
T +33 (0)4 93 16 64 00
www.hotel-negresco-nice.com

Nice Opera House
4-6 rue Saint-François de Paule 06300 Nice
T +33 (0)4 92 17 40 00
www.opera-nice.org

Nouveau Musée National de Monaco (NMNM)
www.nmnm.mc
Villa Paloma 56 boulevard du Jardin Exotique
T +377 98 98 48 60
Closed public holidays & 4 days of the Grand Prix
Open 10am – 6pm (7pm June – Sept)
Villa Sauber 17 avenue Princesse Grace
98000 Monaco
T +377 98 98 91 26
Open 10am – 6pm (7pm June – Sept)

O
Observatoire Astronomique de Nice
boulevard de l'Observatoire 06300 Nice
T +33 (0)4 92 00 30 11
www.oca.eu

P
Palais Lascaris
15 rue Droite 06300 Nice
T +33 (0)4 93 62 72 40
Closed Tues

Picasso Museum
place Mariejol 06600 Antibes
T +33 (0)4 92 90 54 20
www.antibes-juanlespins.com
Closed Mon Open 8am – 12 noon /
2 – 6pm (8 pm July & Aug)
Open all day June – Sept

Polygone
119 avenue des Alpes
06800 Cagnes-sur-Mer
T +33 (0)4 97 02 01 01
www.polygone-riviera.fr

Préau des Enfants
see Espace de l'Art Concret

Prieuré de Vieux-Logis
59 avenue Saint-Barthelem
06100 Nice
T +33 (0)4 93 91 19 10
Closed Tues

R
Russian Orthodox Cathedral
avenue Nicolas II, boulevard Gambetta
06000 Nice
T +33 9 83 94 71 55
Open 10am – 5pm Closed Mon until 1.30 pm

S
Safari Restaurant
1 cours Saleya 06300 Nice
T +33 (0)4 93 80 18 44
Open 12 noon – 11.30 pm

T
Théâtre de la Photographie et de l'Image
27 boulevard Dubouchage 06000 Nice
T + 33 (0)4 97 13 42 01
www.tpi-nice.org
Open 10am – 6pm

V
**Villa Arson - School of Fine Arts and
National Contemporary Art Centre**
20 avenue Stephen Liegeard 06105 Nice
T +33 (0)4 92 07 73 73
www.villa-arson.org
Closed Tues Open 2 – 6 pm (7 pm July & Aug)

Villa Domergue
5 avenue Fiesole 06400 Cannes
T + 33 (0)4 97 06 44 90
Open 11 am – 7 pm (July – Sept)

Villa Grecque Kérylos
Impasse Gustave Eiffel
06310 Beaulieu-sur-Mer
T +33 (0)4 93 01 01 44
www.villa-kerylos.com

Villa Paloma / Villa Sauber
see Nouveau Musée National de Monaco

Volti Museum
Les Musées de La Citadel
Villefranche-sur-Mer
Free entry

Villa Ephrussi de Rothschild
see Fondation Ephrussi de Rothschild

Villa-Musée Jean-Honoré Fragonard
23 boulevard Fragonard 06130 Grasse
T +33(0)4 93 36 01 61
www.museesdegrasse.com
Open 10 am – 7 pm (May – Sept)

Index

Focus.

Goff, Dr Jennifer 217
Goldschmidt, Jeannine de 15
Gorman, Richard 9, 77
Gormley, Antony 78
 Reflection 172
Gottlob, Maurice 173
Goude, Jean-Paul 56
Grasse 137-43, 220
Gray, Eileen 192, 203, **215-19**
 E 1027 216
 Monte Carlo Lantern 210, 217
Greuze, Jean-Baptiste, Head of a Young
 Woman 206
Grimaldi Castle (Cagnes-sur-Mer) 9
Grimaldi Forum (Monaco) 147-9
Grimaldi Palace (Monaco) 151
Guibert, Jean-André 45, 189
Guino, Richard 73, 150
Guttmann, Axel 171

H
Haghigbi, Majid 143
Han dynasty ceramic figures
 Galerie Golconda (St-Paul de Vence)
103-4
 Museum of Asian Arts 34, 35
Harpignies, H.-J. 118
Hartung, Hans **92-6**, 105, 126, 173
 Pyramide d'Argent sur fond
d'Argent Gris 93
 T1976-R39 93
Hazama-Rosolen, Adelia 177
Hélion, Jean 156
Henry, Grace 175
Hermant, André 31
Hippolyte-Lucas, Marie-Félix, Poésie
 Légère 14
Hirst, Damien, Matthew, Mark, Luke and
 John 149
Holy Trinity Church (Nice) 48
Hommage à Ken Saro-Wiwa (Gottfried
 Honegger) 156
Hone, Evie 192
Hone, Nathaniel 123
Honegger, Gottfried 155-8, 159
 Hommage à Ken Saro-Wiwa 156
 Tableau-Relief R1237 157
Horn, Roni 159

Hôtel de Paris (Monaco) 149
Hôtel de Ville (Cannes) 121
Hôtel de Ville (Grasse) 139
Hôtel de Ville (Villefranche-sur-Mer) 124
Hotel Nice Arénas (Nice) 67, 68
Hôtel Saint-Vianney (Le Cannet) 114
Hôtel Windsor (Hôtel des Artistes,
 Nice) 68
Houdon, Jean-Antoine, Comte de
 Valbelle 207

I
Isnard, Vivien 24, 133

J
Jacquet, Alain 19
Jakovsky, Anatole **36**
Jakovsky, Renée 36
Janniot, Alfred Auguste **61-2**
 Apollo 61-3
 Mars 62
 Saturn 63
 Venus 62
Jardin Maréchal Juin 57, 58
Jarry, Michel, Nymphea 59
Jellett, Mainie 192
Jenkins, Paul 24, 76, 175
Jewish Synagogue (Nice) 68-9
JMG Gallery (Mougins) 175
Jouarnais, Jean-Yves 55
Judd, Donald 20, 84, 149

K
Kapoor, Anish 168
Kawiak, Tomek, Habit de Parfumeur 143
Kersalé, Yann 49
 L'Amorse du bleu 52
Kijno, Ladislas 133
Kim En Joong 109
Kisling, Moïse 37, 77
 Landscape 192
Klauke, Jürgen 159
Klein, Yves **20-22**, 24, 52, 133
 Blue Victory of Samothrace 20
 Vénus Bleue 20, 21
 Venus Blue Torso 173
Klementiev, Eugène 67
Kline, Franz 20

Koons, Jeff, Hanging Heart 147
Kreplak, Yaël 55
Kruger, Barbara 20

L
La Chaise de SAB (Sabine Géraudie) 13
La Colombe D'Or Hotel (St-Paul de Vence)
 101-3, 105
La Galerie Lapita (Nice) 44
La Grande Bibliothèque Louis Nucéra
 (Nice) 57-8
La Japonaise (Alberto Magnelli) 176
La Lutte de Jacob et de l'Ange (Marc
 Chagall) 170
La Méditerranée (Volti) 122
La Porte Fausse (Sarkis) 49
La Tête Carrée (Sosno) 57, 58
La Turbie 183-8
La Vénus de St-Paul de Vence (Théo
 Tobiasse) 98
L'Amandier (Pierre Bonnard) 112, 116
Largillière, Nicolas 152
Laurencin, Marie 37, 76
Laurent, Jean-Jacques 133
Lavoir (Mougins) 175
Lavreuse (Pierre-Auguste Renoir) 73-4
Le Broc 135
Le Brocquy, Louis 131-3, 191
 Lemon in the Hand 134
Le Brun, Charles 192
Le Cannet 113-14
Le Corbusier (Charles-Édouard Jeanneret-
 Gris) 173, 217-19
Le Guetteur (Sacha Sosno) 78, 79
Le Musée Municipal (Draguignan) 205
Le Pouce (César Baldaccini) 59, 60
Le Vieux Roi, (Pablo Picasso) 89
Le Vieux-Nice (Nice Old Town) 23-4, 25
Lebasque, Henri 37
Leccia, Ange 49, 52
Léger, Fernand 81-7, 100, 103, 120, 133,
 171, 173, 221
 Composition Murale 84
 Des haut-reliefs en céramique 82-3
 Jardin d'Enfance 83-4
 La Partie de Campagne 86
 Les Acrobats 85
 Les Baigneuses 86-7

Acknowledgements

I wish to thank the many people who assisted me in the research and preparation of this guide. Riviera resident Katherine McCrea Garnier first planted the seed when she observed a gap in the market for an art guide and suggested I was the right person to write it. Flattered, I prepared a first draft which Penny Harris-Healy agreed to read and returned with the most useful editorial suggestions to improve the material. She also took on the arduous task of typing my handwritten manuscript. John Montague, distinguished poet and resident of Nice, kindly agreed to write an introduction, for which I am grateful.

Artisan House of Connemara read my manuscript, apparently liked it and undertook to publish it. Mary Ruddy and Vincent Murphy of Artisan House, ably assisted by Betty Murphy, have since taken infinite pains to ensure that the edited text and selected illustrations have dovetailed in what I hope you will agree is a most attractive synthesis. I deeply appreciate the care and attention they have given this title. I am grateful to Stan Carey for his careful and thorough copy-editing and to Kate Murphy for her proofing and indexing work.

I thank my friend in Brazil, Julio Landmann, artist Mick O'Dea of the *Royal Hibernian Academy* in Dublin, and Olivier Bergesi of *MAMAC* in Nice, for their generous endorsements.

Many other people helped along the way. Firstly I would like to thank those in the French Riviera and in France for their cooperation:

Christian Estrosi, *Deputy of France* and *Mayor of Nice*
Madame Laurence Fournier, *International Relations, Mairie de Cannes*
Anne Dopfer, *Conservateur Général de Patrimoine, Directrice des Musées Nationaux du XXe siècle des Alpes-Maritime*
Jean-Pierre Barbero, *Coordonnateur des Musées,* Nice
Aika Sapone and Laure Matarasso, Nice
Pierre Joannon, *Consul General of Ireland,* Cannes
Madame Gwenaëlle Fossard, *Les Héritiers Matisse,* Issy-Les-Moulineaux
Isabelle Giovacchini and guide, Helen, *Rosary Chapel,* Vence

Acknowledgements

Isabelle Lavarenne, *Photothèque, Musée Matisse,* Nice
François Fernandez, Nice
Carole Lenglet, *Le Musée Bonnard,* Le Cannet
Magali Barsante, *Musée de la Castres,* Le Suquet, Cannes
Cécile Bertran, *Conservatrice des Musées de Cagnes-sur-Mer*
Elsa Hougue, *Responsable de la communication et des Rélations Publiques, Fondacion Hartung-Bergman,* Antibes
Staff of *Picasso Museum*, Antibes
Staff of *Léger Museum,* Biot
Jean-Paul Monery, *Conservateur en chef,* and Josiane Petton, *le Secrétariat, Musée de l'Annonciade,* Saint-Tropez
Elsa Guigo, *Chargée de la Communication et du Mécénat, Espace de l'Art Concret, Château de Mouans,* Mouans-Sartoux
Madame Danielle Roux, *La Colombe d'Or Hotel,* Saint-Paul de Vence
Catherine Weil, *Secrétariat, Musée Chagall,* Nice
Stefany Laurent, *Régie des service, Musée Magnelli, Musée de la Céramique,* Vallauris
Mélissa Mari, *assistante communication, Fragonard Parfumeur,* Grasse
Stéphanie Monnet, *Picasso Administration,* Paris
Françoise Leonelli, *Conservateur, Musée Jean Cocteau, Collection Séverin Wunderman,* Menton
Leila Audouy, *Documentaliste, Agence photographique, RMN-GP,* Paris
Veronique Mamelli, *RMN-GP,* Paris
Tiphaine Leroux, *Administration des Ventes, Réunion des Musées Nationaux – Grand Palais,* Paris
Elizabeth Wassell, Nice
Staff of the various tourist offices throughout the French Riviera, from Menton to Draguignan, who answered my many questions and queries.

Likewise, I thank the following in Ireland and the UK for their assistance:

Anne Madden Le Brocquy, Dublin
Michael Craig-Martin, R.A., London
Siân Phillips, *Account executive, Bridgeman Images,* London

Continued overleaf   237

Nancy Saul, *Design & Artists Copyright Society*, London

Marie Roux, London

Finbarr Connolly, *Rights and Reproduction, East Annexe, National Museum of Ireland,* Dublin

Jim Butler, *Inspirational Arts*, Dublin

Deirdre and Pat Heneghan, Dublin

Catherine and William Earley, Dublin

Patricia and Eoin McGonigal, Dublin

Alex Davis, *Manager*, Adrian Colwell and Emer Marron, *Irish Visual Artists' Royalties Organisation,* Dublin

Patrick T Murphy, *Director*, and Vanessa Moss of the *Royal Hibernian Academy*, Dublin

Susan Cox and Gerard Whelan, *Royal Dublin Society*

Ross Hinds, *Publisher,* Dublin

Caroline and Michael Lillis, Nice and Dublin

Christina Barry, *Artisan House Connemara*, Co. Galway

Lindsey Bacigal, *Aquinas College,* Michigan and Connemara

Joanna McMinn, Belfast

Professor Liam Kelly, Belfast and Cagnes-sur-Mer

Jacquie Moore, *Deputy Art Advisor, Office of Public Works,* Dublin

I wish to express my most grateful thanks to His Excellency, French Ambassador to Ireland, Jean-Pierre Thébault, for kindly agreeing to launch this guide at the *Royal Hibernian Academy* in Ely Place, Dublin, in May 2016. My thanks also go to his staff, Cultural Attaché Frédéric Rauser and his assistant Stéphanie Muchint, who were most helpful and encouraging.

Finally, I wish to acknowledge and thank my wife, Antoinette, who accompanied me on many of my visits to the various galleries and museums, and my son Bryan Murphy and his wife Kathryn Murphy for their valuable assistance with photography.

Patrick J Murphy

May 2016

Image credits

The author and publisher gratefully acknowledge permission to use copyright material in this book. Copyright holders are acknowledged on this page. Every effort has been made to trace and contact copyright holders. If there are any inadvertent omissions we apologise to those concerned, and ask that you contact us so that we can correct any oversight as soon as possible. For contact details please refer to the imprint page (p2) of this book.

Images on the following pages were photographed by Patrick J Murphy:
p 12, 13, 14, 15, 16, 23, 24, 25, 29, 30, 34, 36, 37, 39, 40, 42, 43, 44, 45, 46, 47, 48, 52, 53, 57, 58, 59, 60, 61, 62, 63, 64, 66, 72, 74, 76, 79, 82, 83, 96, 98, 102, 107, 113, 116, 122, 124, 125, 144, 148, 153, 160, 166-7, 182, 183, 184, 185, 186, 188, 190, 194, 195, 196, 211, 212, 223

Cover	**Henri Matisse** *Madame Matisse* 1905 © Succession H. Matisse Photo: François Fernandez	
"	**Aristide Maillol** *La Nymphe* 1931 L'Annonciade, musée de Saint-Tropez	
"	**Anne Madden** *Empyrius* 1999 © courtesy of the artist Photo: Claude Germain	
"	**Museum of Asian Arts** Kenzō Tange (architect) Photo: Patrick J Murphy	
p2	**Mary Swanzy** *South of France landscape* (detail) c.1915 © Estate of Mary Swanzy Photo: Bryan Murphy	
p12	**Sabine Géraudie** *La Chaise de SAB* 2014 Photo: Patrick J Murphy	
p14	**Niki de Saint Phalle** *The Trumpeter* 1999 Photo: Patrick J Murphy	
p17	**Andy Warhol** *Dollar Sign* 1981 © The Andy Warhol Foundation for the Visual Arts, Inc. ARS New York / IVARO Dublin, 2016	
p18	**Alexander Calder** *Théâtre de Nice* 1970 © Calder Foundation, New York. ARS New York / IVARO Dublin, 2016	
p19	**Morris Louis** *Alpha Lambda* 1962 © Maryland College Institute of Art. All Rights Reserved. ARS New York IVARO Dublin, 2016	
p21	**Yves Klein** *Vénus Bleue* 1960 © Estate of Yves Klein, ADAGP Paris / IVARO Dublin, 2016	
p22	**Niki de Saint Phalle** *Nana Noire* 1966 © The Niki Charitable Art Foundation. ADAGP Paris / IVARO Dublin, 2016	
p22	**Bernar Venet** *Ligne Indéterminée* 1983 © ADAGP Paris / IVARO Dublin, 201	
p23	**Bernar Venet** *Arc 11505* 1988 Photo: Patrick J Murphy	
p23	**Bernar Venet** *Neuf Lignes Obliques* 2010 Photo: Patrick J Murphy	
p27	**Henri Matisse** *Madame Matisse* 1905 © Succession H. Matisse Photo: François Fernandez	
p28	**Henri Matisse** *Nature morte aux grenades* 1947 © Succession H. Matisse Photo: François Fernandez	
p32	**Marc Chagall** *The Creation of the World* Chagall ®/© ADAGP Paris / IVARO Dublin, 2016	
p35	**Unknown** *La Courtisane à la jupe bleue* 1830 © Coll. Musée de la Castre, Cannes Photo: © B.Holsnyder	
p49	**Sarkis** *La Porte Fausse* 2007 Photo: Vincent Murphy	
p50	**Michael Craig-Martin** *Cascade d'objets* 2007 © courtesy of the artist Photo: Michael Craig-Martin	
p51	**Jaume Plensa** *Conversation à Nice* 2007 Photo: Vincent Murphy	
p52	**Gunda Förster** *Blue, hommage au bleu d'Yves Klein* 2007 Photo: Patrick J Murphy	
p58	**Sacha Sosno** (sculptor) **Yves Bayard** (architect) *La Tête Carrée* 2009 Photo: Patrick J Murphy	
p59	**César Baldaccini** *Le Pouce* 1965 Photo: Patrick J Murphy	
p61	**Alfred Auguste Janniot** *Apollo* 1957 Photo: Patrick J Murphy	
p62	**Alfred Auguste Janniot** *Venus, Mars, Saturn* 1957 Photo: Patrick J Murphy	
p64	**Michelangelo** *David* 1957 Photo: Patrick J Murphy	
p72	**Pierre-Auguste Renoir** *Venus Victrix (Madame Renoir)* 1916 Photo: Patrick J Murphy	
p74	**Pierre-Auguste Renoir** Relief portraits 1918 Photo: Patrick J Murphy	
p74	Renoir's wheelchair beside his easel, paints and brushes Photo: Patrick J Murphy	
p75	**Pierre-Auguste Renoir** *Les Grandes Baigneuses* 1887 Photo: © RMN-GP Michel Urtado	
p79	**Sacha Sosno** (sculptor) Yves Bayard (architect) *Le Guetteur* 2015 Photo: Patrick J Murphy	
p80	**Fernand Léger** *Les Loisirs sur Fond Rouge* 1949 © Estate of Fernand Léger, ADAGP Paris / IVARO Dublin 2016 Photo: © RMN-GP Gérard Blot	
p83	**Fernand Léger** *Des haut-reliefs en céramique* 1955 Photo: Patrick J Murphy	
p85	**Fernand Léger** *Les Loisirs sur Fond Rouge* 1949 © Estate of Fernand Léger, ADAGP Paris / IVARO Dublin 2016 Photo: © RMN-GP Gérard Blot	
p86	**Fernand Léger** *Les Baigneuses* 1980 © Estate of Fernand Léger, ADAGP Paris / IVARO Dublin 2016 Photo: © RMN-GP Gérard Blot	
p88	**Pablo Picasso** *Le Vieux Roi* 1959 © Succession Picasso / DACS London 2016 Photo: Bryan Murphy	

ADAGP Société des Auteurs dans les Arts Graphiques et Plastiques **ARS** Artists Rights Society **CIAC** Centre International d'Art Contemporain
DACS Design & Artists Copyright Society **IVARO** Irish Visual Artists Rights Organisation **RMN-GNGP** Réunion des Musées Nationaux et du Grand Palais

Continued overleaf 239

Image credits

p91	**Pablo Picasso** *La Joie de Vivre* 1946 © Succession Picasso / DACS London 2016 / Musée Picasso, Antibes / Bridgeman Images
p92,94	**Fondation Hartung-Bergman** © (all rights reserved), p.94 Image of couple photo: François Walch
p96	**Raymond Peynet** *Lovers* 1950 Photo: Patrick J Murphy
p98	**Théo Tobiasse** *La Vénus de St-Paul de Vence* 2008 Photo: Patrick J Murphy
p101	**La Colombe d'Or Hotel** © Images courtesy La Colombe d'Or Hotel
p104	**Robert Delaunay** *Femme à l'Ombrelle* 1913 © Estate of Robert Delaunay, L'Annonciade, musée de Saint-Tropez
p106	**Henri Matisse** Stained glass (detail) Matisse Chapel © Succession H. Matisse Photo: François Fernandez
p107	**Henri Matisse** Matisse Chapel entrance © Succession H. Matisse Photo: François Fernandez
p110-111	**Henri Matisse** Matisse Chapel © Succession H. Matisse Photo: François Fernandez
p112	**Pierre Bonnard** *L'Amandier* 1930 © Estate of Pierre Bonnard, Musée Bonnard, Le Cannet / ADAGP Paris / IVARO Dublin, 2016
p115	**Unknown** *Tiki-poteau de Té Atoua* © Coll. Musée de la Castre, Cannes Photo: © Claude Germain
p117	**Pierre Bonnard** *Nu devant profil* 1917 © Estate of Pierre Bonnard, Musée Bonnard, Le Cannet / ADAGP Paris / IVARO Dublin, 2016
p122	**Volti** *La Méditerranée* 1961 Photo: Patrick J Murphy
p124	**Volti** Female nude Photo: Patrick J Murphy
p125	**Volti** *The Three Graces* Photo: Patrick J Murphy
p130	**Anne Madden** *Empyrius* (detail) 1999 © courtesy of the artist Photo: Claude Germain
p132	**Anne Madden** *Empyrius* 1999 © courtesy of the artist Photo: Claude Germain
p134	**Louis Le Brocquy** *Lemon in the Hand* 1973 © Pierre Le Brocquy Photo: Bryan Murphy
p136	**Jean-Honoré Fragonard** *Jeune fille délivrant un oiseau de sa cage* 1775 © Fragonard Parfumeur, Grasse
p141	**Marguerite Gérard** *La Bonne Nouvelle* 1798 © Fragonard Parfumeur, Grasse
p154	**Château de Mouans** © Photo: François Fernandez
p156	**Gottfried Honegger** *Hommage à Ken Saro-Wiwa* 1996 © Espace d'Art Concret, Donation Albers-Honnegger
p157	**Espace d'Art Concret** *Préau des Enfants* Gigon/Guyer (architects) © Photo: François Fernandez
p158	**François Morellet** *Ligne horizontale passant sur trois carrés* 1974 © ADAGP Paris / IVARO Dublin, 2016 © Photo: François Fernandez
p170	**Marc Chagall** *La Lutte de Jacob et de l'Ange* 1966 Chagall ®/© ADAGP Paris / IVARO Dublin, 2016
p174	**Mary Swanzy** *South of France landscape* c.1915 © Estate of Mary Swanzy Photo: Bryan Murphy
p176	**Alberto Magnelli** *La Japonaise* 1914 © Estate of Alberto Magnelli, ADAGP Paris / IVARO Dublin, 2016
p180	**Pablo Picasso** *War* 1954 © Succession Picasso / DACS London 2016 Musée National Picasso La Guerre et la Paix, Vallauris / Bridgeman Images
p194-195	**Musée Jean Cocteau** Rudy Ricciotti (architect) Photo: Patrick J Murphy
p196	**Jean Cocteau** Entrance to the Bastion Museum Photo: Patrick J Murphy
p198	**Pierre Bonnard** *Nu devant la cheminée* 1919 © Estate of Pierre Bonnard, Musée Bonnard, Le Cannet / ADAGP Paris / IVARO Dublin, 2016
p200	**André Derain** *Westminster Palace* 1907 © Estate of André Derain, ADAGP Paris / IVARO Dublin, 2016
p201	**Georges Braque** *Paysage de l'Estaque* 1906 © Estate of Georges Braque, L'Annonciade, musée de Saint-Tropez, ADAGP Paris / IVARO Dublin, 2016
p202	**Aristide Maillol** *La Nymphe* 1931 © Estate of Aristide Maillol, L'Annonciade, musée de Saint-Tropez
p204	**Walter Pfeiffer** *Lavender field* © Photo: Walter Pfeiffer
p210	**Eileen Gray** Monte Carlo Lantern 1923 Image courtesy National Museum of Ireland
p216	**Eileen Gray** & **Jean Badovici** *E 1027* 1929 Image courtesy National Museum of Ireland
p217	**Eileen Gray** Monte Carlo Lantern 1923 Image courtesy National Museum of Ireland

ADAGP Société des Auteurs dans les Arts Graphiques et Plastiques **ARS** Artists Rights Society **CIAC** Centre International d'Art Contemporain
DACS Design & Artists Copyright Society **IVARO** Irish Visual Artists Rights Organisation **RMN - GNGP** Réunion des Musées Nationaux et du Grand Palais